FOREWORD

When I first met Rachel, it was in consultation for breast reconstruction. As a Plastic and Reconstructive Surgeon, I often meet patients for the first time in unfortunate circumstances. Rachel was no exception, having recently been diagnosed with breast cancer.

Rachel left a marked impression on me in the first meeting, She presented with an energy that drew people towards her. She was bright, inquisitive, and met all challenges with a sense of humour, a positive attitude and a hunger for knowledge.

At the time I was aware that she was dealing with more issues than her cancer diagnosis, but it wasn't until she honoured me by sending me an early version of this book that I truly appreciated all she had been experiencing at that time. Learning the whole of her story, I felt sincere empathy and the utmost respect for her approach to the challenges she has faced.

Rachel has clearly not written this book looking for sympathy, and you will certainly not hear her complaining or moaning about the cards she has been dealt in life.

True to her nature, her book is about learning. It's about emerging from a difficult situation having grown and becoming better than you were before.

As she wended her way through the first crisis, it became immediately and increasingly clear to Rachel that she needed to take complete charge of her life, and take charge she did. In some ways, this new direction was derailed by her cancer diagnosis, but the diagnosis also brought her to a new depth of understanding — one that would allow her to appreciate the beauty of the everyday that she was normally too busy to acknowledge.

This understanding rippled into the world around her, leading to a newly honed perception. She came to identify the reasons for her husband's behavioural issues, leading to growth and healing he formerly hadn't known he needed. Now, Rachel's understanding and perception are leading to opportunity in a whole new world.

What I have found most incredible about Rachel's journey, is that she didn't just use these experiences to help understand herself, but to understand others; to help not just herself, but also others.

As a Surgeon, I see every day how attitude affects the quality of a person's life, their surgical journey and the overall long-lasting impact of their cancer diagnosis. In this respect, Rachel's attitude and positive energy truly impressed me. From the moment of her diagnosis, she looked forward. She met challenges and obstacles of her treatment and life with grace and openness. She chose to find the pleasure and joy in the life that surrounded her. She may always have appreciated a sunny day, but from then on she fully immersed herself in that sunny day. She moved back to the UK, little family in tow, and they are all thriving.

The title "How to Wear a Silver Lining" is apt, as Rachel takes any unfortunate situation and finds the hope and the goodness within.

With any luck, readers will be encouraged to look for the good in any situation, and even more so, to create the good.

- Dr. Mary-Helen Mahoney, MD, FRCSC

HOW TO WEAR A SILVER LINING

RACHEL LINDLEY LOVE

Quantity sales.
Special discounts are available on quantity purchases by corporations, associations, and others.

For details, contact the author via www.rachellindleylove.com
or contact the publisher at the address below

Violet King Publishing
PO Box 2632
Garibalidi Highlands
British Columbia
V0N 1T0
Canada

HOW TO WEAR A SILVER LINING

RACHEL LINDLEY LOVE

Dedicated to Shirin Teifouri, whose boundless encouragement
and support inspired me to write my story.

TABLE OF CONTENTS

INTRODUCTION

SILVER-LINED FINERY

The beginning of a fall — that excruciating moment when we know that gravity will have its way with us — we see what's coming but we are utterly helpless to prevent it. Unable to breathe, stomach lurching, body like cement, brain exploding like a Catherine wheel.

Our minds leap through the circus hoops of "Ahhh!" and "Oh NO!" as the inevitable occurs. Time slows, the fall at once instantaneous and drawn out. And then we land centre stage in an unread and unrehearsed play, an ominous knowing that the act to follow will be disconcerting at best, terrifying at worst. This unsettling realisation is rapidly chased with an overdose of uncertainty. The scope of the damage unassessed and impossible to consider from the whirling discombobulation of a mind in shock. There we stand, alone, yet feeling like a thousand eyes are trained upon us, watching, waiting to see how bad the fallout will actually be.

Assessing the consequences is phase two. Once released from the trance of shock and disbelief we must determine what is broken. Can we get up? Are the injuries life-threatening? And then, will recovery be possible?

After a life-shattering event, these simple determinations can be overwhelming. You must learn all the ways your world has been impacted. Treading gingerly and wisely into this unnavigated imposing new world is perhaps how we imagine we will deal with the repercussions of a trauma. Perhaps we imagine we can make clear and rational decisions, that we will say and do the right things, as we might under ordinary circumstances. But the reality is often quite different. A chemical cannonball is released into the body and making the right choices is akin to being able to stand zen-like and motionless in a wind tunnel. Sometimes the simple act of just getting through a day without dropping to your knees is all you can muster. Creating your new reality is phase three of the fall and the way you shape that world will very much depend on how you decide to pick up the pieces, if you pick them up at all.

On an ordinary evening in 2018, in the west end of the sparkling metropolis of Toronto, Canada, a small house party was underway. My party, with my neighbours and Jesse, my husband of thirteen years. I was in my sociable element, surrounded by people I knew not only because of our close proximity, but who had become good friends in our nine years of living there.

That night was when the fabric of my world first began to rip apart. But while the tear struck me as shocking, as if it had come with no warning signs, in retrospect I see it was not entirely inadvertent. It was not the force majeure it had initially appeared to be.

Because Jesse had made a decision that night to see what would happen if he pushed the boundaries of his reality, dangled his life over the edge of reason. And the results were showstopping. Not showstopping in the way you're enthralled and in awe at what you're witnessing, but in the way you stop and gawk in disbelief that someone survived a death-defying car crash. And ultimately we both had to face the reality that aspects of this decision were not as contrary to his nature as we'd thought.

That night Jesse ignited a chain reaction of devastating consequences that almost ended his own life. He wreaked havoc on an innocent bystander who would be permanently scarred, and he left his family devastated. Jesse's brain was malfunctioning for reasons that weren't initially clear. Ordinarily a kind and tender man, but also a man who liked to metaphorically play with fire on occasion. A man who liked to drink in all that life had to offer and engage with it full throttle. A man with a golden heart but a curiosity that stepped over the boundaries of safe and reasonable exploration. Maybe because he was so capable physically and revelled in a challenge, maybe because he had too much testosterone, maybe because in the excitement of a moment and under poor advisement he made a terrible decision.

Falling into this turbulent new era of our lives, we seemed to be lurching from one day to the next, gasping for breath the moment we slammed into the waking screech of our alarm clocks. During that year a string of days might pass that offered relief, a precious life raft of reprieve drifting gently by. But just as soon as we had grabbed hold of hope we found ourselves gulping in a suffocating wave of more life-changing news. Like a gruesome, foreboding pendulum I learned my own mortality was ticking over me at an untimely and frightening speed. Would this year be the last year I would get to celebrate my child's birthday? Would this year be the last year I could nuzzle into my dog's unruly fur? Would this year be the last year of every single experience I would ever have?

Jesse's actions that night ended our marriage. But some months after the wreckage, when we were faced with my own mortality, his actions repaired our marriage. Because that's what marriage is: the drop, the pieces, the blame, the anger and the effort it takes to put it back together. Which isn't always worth it. But sometimes it is.

I'm reminded of Kintsugi, the centuries-old Japanese art of repairing broken pottery by mending the breakage with a metallic lacquer, normally gold or silver. Kintsugi, which literally means golden (kint) joinery (sugi) celebrates the breakage and embraces the moment of impact as an opportunity to beautify something ordinary. The metallic lacquer makes no attempt to conceal the cracks but rather gloriously highlights their uniqueness.

It's also a poetic metaphor for the art of embracing one's own damage. It reminds us to stop seeking perfection and instead to see the strength and beauty in our brokenness. Repair, yes, but don't expect things to be exactly as they were before. We are all destined to be broken in one way or another and, if we choose, we can use the experience to birth something new, something stronger, better and far more interesting.

Although the art of kintsugi refers to the metallic mending on the exterior of the object, I chose to visualize my own repair with a silver lining. The etymology of a silver lining is from Milton's Comus, which he wrote in 1634, though the term "every cloud has a silver lining" didn't appear until 1849, but given my fashion stylist sensibility, I see it as the silver lining of an exquisite and beloved piece of clothing.

If my life was ever to shatter into pieces again, I would be able to see that silver lining and know that I had done this work before, that I had the guidance of prior experience and a wellspring of resilience to call upon. But more than simply remembering to find beauty in our shattering experiences, I wanted to somehow drink in that silver lining, to carry a more intimate reminder of the power of looking for the gift in tragedy. I wanted to wear the glow of hope, so I imagined myself wrapped in it, wearing it as if the magical power of optimism would seep into my being.

In just such an evolution I had faced a crisis in my previous marriage, four years before I met Jesse. I had lived through a betrayal that rippled through every one of my relationships at the time with heart-wrenching consequences, and created a financial situation that sucker-punched me right in the gut.

But it was that situation that helped me develop the mental fortitude to survive what was to come. It was that experience that provided the perspective I would need down the road, and had been an abrupt introduction to the necessity of finding a silver lining. A dramatic testing ground to see if I could reach above the clouds and see the reflection of the moon shining in a beacon of hope. It was Milton dropping off the idea and then letting me fine-tune its meaningful impact decades on.

After all of these trials, which you will soon learn the details of, this silver lining has become part of my being, by practice and discipline and a constant regulation of my inner chatter. I meditate (poorly), I journal, I re-frame disappointment, I challenge myself to judge less and expand my empathy, I count to ten when I feel like lashing out, I remember to breathe, and I value rest. I acknowledge and even embrace my harsh inner critic and try my best to respond to her with kindness, knowing she needs it most when she is fierce.

As I went through crisis after crisis in my marriages and my life, I became adept at finding silver linings. Like a star seasoned traveller I could navigate the storms and not be blown off course as quickly and easily as I used to be. I learned to set my inner compass in the direction of hope and faith, however you define it. I don't do any of it perfectly, and so I fail and fail and fail. But kintsugi and silver linings remind me of my ability to choose a different reality, to pause and bear witness to life rather than being swept away by it. Through the art of self-awareness, reckoning with our demons, embracing our wounds and understanding the grace that lies beyond the change-agents of trauma there is an existence more glorious than we could ever imagine.

This book is the gallery that holds my kintsugi masterpiece. The journey itself is broken into three parts: The Shattering, The Fragments and The Repair. The hallways through the gallery are filled with clouds — hazy clouds that sometimes seem so dense you cannot pass through, other times they are light and ethereal, magical and dreamy. Some hallways are adorned with clouds like fairy-lights, twinkling and flickering, showing you the way. Others are ominous and stormy, threatening and disturbing. But if you can see the silver lining in every incarnation then your journey will be more joyful, more delightfully unexpected and ultimately sublime. As you travel with me you may find your own shattered parts. I hope that together we will hold the pieces with reverence and with a depth of compassion only the deeply broken understand.

If you find yourself reflected in these pages then know that I'm with you, if not in body, then entwined in the psychic wounds of dark experience and holding a space for you in the kintsugi gallery. This holy space of the broken and masterfully repaired. Let's begin to break — then pick up our pieces.

PART I:
THE SHATTERING

Only in the surreal realm of the unconscious could I have imagined our lives so instantaneously and incontrovertibly altered.

Chapter 1

PARTY DRESS

Looking back, it still feels like the pages of a Steven King novel playing out in my memory. Our ordinary lives were suddenly and violently hijacked by a raging, sinister character.

This character had previously dominated a handful of small scenes with his wild and unpredictable behaviour, but I hoped he had been edited out of my script.

If I could use denial like an eraser, mopping up the ugly parts of him, making him vanish from the pages of my life, then I would be back in control of the story, wouldn't I? What I should have remembered from my art school days was that when you use an eraser with enough vigour, there is always a thick gummy blackened debris that inconveniently scars the page.

Unbeknownst to me, he would soon appear in chapter upon chapter of sullied pages that would be impossible to erase. In the space of minutes, those chapters rushed into formation, and we began a trajectory that would take us on a blindfolded roller coaster ride that careened into months of uncertainty and life-changing consequences.

It was the day after our tenth anniversary, Friday night, November 2, 2018. My husband and I had a lot to celebrate. Jesse was relishing his rock-star status in his new job; we had a gorgeous, historic loft in the west end of Toronto and were blessed to be surrounded by wonderful neighbours. Our nine-year-old daughter, Everleigh, was happy and healthy, and Jesse and I were soaring into middle age without so much as an aching joint. I felt rich because of all this and so much more that was good in our lives, and I was mindful to acknowledge my privilege and the opportunities that came with it.

Our apartment was abuzz with the movement of music and people. An impromptu gathering had shifted from another loft in our building to ours and picked up random neighbours along the way — the type of gathering that community living often gives way to, and my favourite way to socialize. My immediate neighbours would charitably tolerate the occasional blast of music being played too loudly; perhaps they knew how the power of a certain song could unlock our emotional vaults. Accompanied by friends either uninhibited or drunk, we wailed to the music and flung our limbs about like we were Beyoncé's back-up crew. It was a night of unleashed performance, interspersed with laughter and delightful conversation.

Around 10 p.m. I ushered Everleigh off to bed, a night-owl like her dad. She protested at not being allowed to stay up. Her bedroom was located on the second storey of our loft, tucked at the end of a long hallway that showcased her gallery of artwork. Her white and pale lilac room with its dramatic vaulted ceiling was her sanctuary, and one of the few private spaces in our open-plan apartment. In the ensuing half-hour she would periodically appear at the top of the stairs, quietly bearing witness to the playground below. I ushered her back to bed with a cuddle and kiss, but if I had known what was about to unfold, I would have locked her in her room with a double bolt.

At around 11 p.m. our guests trailed back to their own homes, and I found myself pleasantly alone amongst the empty beer cans and lipstick-stained wine glasses. My husband must be on the front stoop, I figured, the common gathering place for smokers to socialize. I was gathering glasses and enjoying the contentment of a convivial evening when he burst through the front door like a cyclone — my husband Jesse, wild-eyed and pacing, unrecognizable.

He was striding back and forth in the small entryway beside the kitchen. I spoke carefully, calmly, gingerly, acutely aware that I was confronting a volatile altered state. "Jesse, let's take a seat for a minute."

I warily guided him to the barstool in front of the kitchen island. As I manoeuvred his body, his seething anxiety was palpable. He was ordinarily imperturbable, sometimes annoyingly unexcitable. I had never seen this Jesse before. I tried to curb his frenzied movements, asking him to breathe, put his hands on the countertop, connect with something, ground himself, as if whatever was happening in his body was behaving like a bucking electrified wire. He sat for just a moment and then mumbled and paced and fled through the front door. Now infected with his panic, my mind began to whip through possibilities. It was obvious he had taken something, something more than alcohol, and I figured one of our guests had shared something with him at the party.

My husband is six-foot-four. He has a military crew-cut hairstyle and a menacing-looking scar over his left eye. He did in fact spend seven years in the Canadian reserves, training and teaching heavy weapons. He looks and sounds the part, with a deep commanding voice that makes you pay attention. He is also aware of the space he occupies and the way his voice can be intimidating. He is tender and gentle and laughs easily. He's the first to play with our daughter when she wants to paint his nails or do a yoga challenge. He makes me coffee exactly the way I like it and folds our laundry as if it's made of fine silk. He is obliging, magnanimous, personable and charming. In that moment, however, he had become a terrifying imposter I couldn't reach.

The next few hours unfolded in the freakish and divergent way time does in a crisis, inexplicably morphing from slow-motion to high-speed. Time feels like its pages are being ripped from the book of order, savagely yanked from the spine and thrown overhead as the reader looks on in disbelief, unable to make events flow through logical and rhythmic succession. Time, this basic tenet of what gives us structure and helps us makes sense of the world — it gets shredded, it collapses then expands like it has taken on some other-dimensional quality. I had dissociated, and was now viewing the situation unfolding as if it were happening to someone else. I had become the spectator. My body was trapped in a quagmire of nonsensical events and my mind couldn't tether itself to safety.

There was a ruckus outside our door. I stepped into the lobby to investigate and found a group of people gathered beside the elevator, amongst them my fellow British neighbours, Mark and Suzanne. Suzanne was wrapped in her bathrobe, as if she'd been woken by the disturbance. Her husband was alarmed, frenzied. He dashed down the stairwell.

In the commotion from the crowd at the elevators a man yelled, "I don't know, but that guy just attacked my friend! He just ... ATTACKED her!"

With what seemed like a mixture of pity and fear, Suzanne spotted me in the crowd. She had become privy to information that hadn't yet reached me, and as a result appeared by my side, preparing to prop me up. She tenderly guided me back to my loft and perched uneasily on the edge of my kitchen barstool. I busied myself tidying the countertop, the cluttered debris of scattered bottles, cans and glasses echoing the tangle of knots that was taking root in my gut. Suzanne was talking, her voice a haze of sounds interfering with my panicked inner dialogue. She was trying to anchor me, to soothe me, to reassure me.

Mark came unannounced through the doorway, an unwitting harbinger of life unravelling. "I'm sorry," he said. "I'm really sorry."

I couldn't make sense of what was happening. Who was he talking to, why was he telling me he was sorry all the time? What the fuck was happening?

"He's just attacked a woman. I don't know what's going on. He's off his head. What has he done? Did he take something?"

Nausea began to swell. Mark's words stabbing me like a paralyzing anaesthetic, I was frozen in place. Suzanne tried her best to be the antidote: "We don't know what's happening, so let's not jump to conclusions. Shall I go and find out?"

A bleak disquietude had drifted into our apartment. Trepidation was surging through my body and my nervous system felt like it would short-circuit.

Mark appeared and disappeared, each time bringing with him reports of the unfolding pandemonium outside. Jesse was on the street below, rampaging like a wild-eyed, frenzied cadre of Vikings. I wanted to slam the door shut and bolt it, with the gravity and futility of trying to stop a tsunami from barrelling towards me.

"He's walking over cars, and he just ran into a moving bus. I'm so sorry."

My brain regurgitated his words. Walking over cars? What the hell does he mean? And ran into a bus, how do you run into a bus?! Oh God. You don't run into a bus. At least, you don't walk away from running into a bus. Why is he telling me he's sorry again?

Suzanne, clutching her bathrobe tighter around herself, spoke words like spun cotton; they were soft and gentle, but fuzzy. I couldn't bring them into focus in my head. "I just saw the woman he attacked. She looks fine. I'm sure it'll be fine. He wouldn't hurt a fly."

For a moment I felt a tiny pang of relief. She's ok; Suzanne just told me she's ok. She must be ok? Then I heard sirens. Screaming, screeching sirens, and the apartment was soaked in glaring red lights.

Mark arrived, slightly out of breath. This time he looked agonized. "He's been arrested. They took him away. They wouldn't say where. But there were two fire trucks, three cop cars and an ambulance. I'm sorry. I don't know what to say."

His words took hold and hauled me into a savage turbulence. I felt nauseated and lightheaded. I needed to sit down. I needed this to stop. I needed someone to put the pieces together for me.

Time was unfolding in a nebulous anarchic manner. You're moving forward through time, yet also watching it stand still, as if this man-made construction has no power anymore, as if it too gave up logic and surrendered to something bigger. When time starts behaving wildly it's the first rule of 'You're Fucked'

- nothing is going to make sense anymore, nothing is going to follow the rules, nothing is going to conform in this disorienting new world.

I don't remember when the two police officers appeared in my kitchen. My kitchen, uncharacteristically littered with the debris of partygoers. I was scrambling to tidy up, as if I were trying to prove to them: This is actually an orderly home; all is well here; no we don't drink that much; there were other people here; this isn't how it usually is.

"I can see he's been violent with you," said one of the officers.

The shock of his words surged through me. How could he assume such a thing? What the hell made him think that? As a cop wasn't he supposed to not jump to conclusions? It was Suzanne who broke the silence, quickly piecing together what the officer was observing, "No, no. That's just mascara."

I had been wiping tears from my eyes after Mark's last report. I had been totally unaware of how I looked — black streaks war-like across my cheeks. The brief exchange had slammed me into the moment. I could see how this was going to go,

'Get a grip,' I told myself. 'Speak slowly and calmly. Show them you're in control. Think. Think. Think.'

They scribbled notes in little black notepads, peppering me with questions. "Who else lives here? Who else was at the party? Were there kids here? Do you have kids? What does your husband do for a living? How long have you lived here? How much have you had to drink? How much has he had to drink? Do you own this place?" My behaviour was being meticulously scrutinized. Please God, I hoped Everleigh had fallen asleep and wasn't witness to any of this. How would I explain what was going on?

When their interrogation ended, I asked, "Where is my husband right now? What exactly has happened? Can you please tell me what's going on?"

They couldn't. They were in my kitchen trying to gather information, not to help me make sense of the deranged, lawless night. They left.

Suzanne and I sat in the aftershock and she congratulated me on keeping it together as the cops sat there wielding their pens and judgments. The lucid façade had taken such a colossal effort; now that they had gone I felt a burgeoning hysteria. Suzanne had been sitting in my kitchen for hours. It was around 2 a.m. when she left. We lived in a tight-knit community. We looked out for each other.

"I feel sick." I had muttered those words several times already.

Where the hell was Jesse?

It occurred to me there might be information on our local social media page. To my horror, a thread had appeared with photographs of the commotion on the street and a string of comments about "this monster" in our neighbourhood. One person gave an account of what Jesse had done to a helpless woman, an innocent passer-by. I felt my knees buckle as I read the comments. But others requested the post be taken down, that it was inappropriate to be voyeuristic, especially when this individual was obviously having a mental health crisis. How could they be talking about my husband? How could he have hurt a woman — a WOMAN?!

At around 2:30 a.m. I remembered I had one of the officer's cards. I called the station number. I was connected to a female officer.

"Can you please give me some information about where my husband might be and what has happened?" I spelled out his name and gave her our address.

"Well, I can't really tell you. I'm not supposed to tell you anything …"

I was screaming inside. Why the fuck wouldn't anyone tell me what had happened?! I stayed calm, knowing that any kind of hysteria on my part was going to end the conversation completely.

"Okay … that's fine, but can you at least tell me where he is?"

"'They took him to St. Joe's for evaluation."

"Evaluation?"

"Yeah, look, I shouldn't be telling you anything. But what kind of a house do you live in anyway? Have you got kids? How many? Where was your kid while all this was going down? Is this something that's happened before?"

My ears were ringing as the blood rushed around my head. What was she talking about?!

"Look, I'll tell you this," she continued. "Your husband is lucky to be alive and the charges against him are very serious. I have to go."

My thoughts began to pirouette like characters in a macabre and surreal circus. I hung up the phone and the nausea took over.

Chapter 2

IN COSTUME

7 A.M.

I vomited, spewing up the chemical dump of cortisol that had been careening through my bloodstream since the night before.

Now what? Now what do I do? How do I tell Everleigh I don't really know where Daddy is, or exactly why he's not here? How would I explain away my trembling hands and puffy eyes? The kid was sagacious, with a finely tuned intuition that I knew wouldn't be placated with a fabricated story. When she awoke she asked me about what I hoped she hadn't seen. "Mommy, why was Daddy acting all weird last night?"

My body was in distress. For hours upon end it had been slowly losing control. My mind had tried to create order from chaos, but without sleep, thoughts were now fully commandeered by panic. I felt ragged and debilitated from shockwave after shockwave of horror. My child stood in front of me with the nervous anxiety of someone who knows that there is a landmine in every direction of inquiry. "I don't know," I said softly. "Are you hungry?"

I fixed her breakfast. I was momentarily grateful for the order of routine and the need for purposeful movement. I had that shaky, adrenaline-fueled, sleep-deprived, unsteady feeling that wouldn't allow me to eat. I drank some water with lemon and kept myself moving: Clean the kitchen. Take a shower.

Brush my hair. Make the bed. Keep. Moving. Forward. I was outrunning the madness, forcing the mayhem into structured, orderly tasks. I called the police station. Maybe I would get a different officer — one who would be a little more forthcoming, a little less judgmental.

My husband was "detained," they told me, in the courthouse downtown. He had been taken to the local hospital for assessment as his behaviour had been violent and erratic, then once released, he was jailed.

A neighbour arrived at my door. "Are you okay?" she asked.

I didn't know how to respond, other than with a mumble and an uncomfortable shuffle, intending to imply I was busy.

She told me a man who'd been at our party, Lewis, had also been behaving strangely the night before. "I heard that Lewis was running down the hallway last night, half naked, like his hair was on fire!" she continued. "His wife tackled him and locked him inside their loft. Apparently they took some magic mushrooms. They must've been cut with something bad — I mean I've never heard of them doing anything like that to people. Are you sure you're okay?"

A rage came over me when I heard the critical piece of information that had been missing. He had taken magic mushrooms.

My anger began catapulting me out of an overwhelming sense of helplessness. I was furious and felt my heart armouring up.

The man I had married was the type of man who liked to push boundaries, but impulsive risk-taking can quickly transform into recklessness. My innately responsible and cautious temperament had been intrigued — captivated, actually — by Jesse's spontaneous behaviour. I was duped by the Hollywood trope that heroes dressed as daring pilots and brave explorers. Manly soldiers and sexy naval officers were exciting, wild and untameable and proud of it. But those characters of romance novels are not the characters you see shacking up and settling down. Under the weight of daily responsibilities, Jesse's spontaneity had morphed into a characteristic that was sometimes unsettling and unreliable.

But like all human beings, Jesse is much more multidimensional than a Hollywood character, and his behaviour that night was an anomaly. He isn't a cliché and doesn't conform to the neat little boxes we attempt to organize people into. At least not the neat little boxes my generation and those before me had constructed. Jesse was flawed, as we all are. People are neither "good" nor "bad". They are both. We are all dimensional and complex, each with our own set of unique experiences that shape our world view, form our opinions and predispose us to certain behaviours. Jesse is deeply soulful and will cry unashamedly at sappy commercials. He loves nature and is profoundly grateful for the simple things in life. He shows up for his friends at any hour of the day and will go out of his way to lend a helping hand to a neighbour. Jesse couldn't be boxed into a role, unsatisfying as that is. None of us can.

But Jesse had made choices over the years that had calcified some of our love and created cracks in the trust we had built. He had concocted his own story that he wasn't good enough for me and that he should therefore push me away before I had the opportunity to break his heart. I had seen glimpses of that narrative and, at times when too much alcohol had taken hold of him, I had become the real-life villain in his head. A cold, uncaring wife who had never really loved him. He had punished me unkindly for being this woman — a woman who didn't exist, one I couldn't relate to, and who was not me.

He played a never-ending loop in his head that he loved me more than I loved him. He looked for evidence of it, in small ways and big. The most innocuous of gestures would be twisted through his storyline, leaving me exasperated and depleted. There wasn't enough "evidence" in our fourteen-year relationship substantial enough to convince him of my love for him. He wouldn't, or couldn't, let it in.

My frustration had grown over time, and trying to get through to him was akin to the experience of engaging with a conspiracy theorist; the more I tried to convince him, the more he clung to his theory. Eventually my frustration had become resentment. There was nothing I could say or do that was reassuring enough, kind enough, gentle enough or simply enough. I was tired of trying to prove myself, so I stopped. And it changed everything.

We had fought over his story of me and I had reached a point of surrender some months before this hellish day arrived. I had learned to separate myself from his fiction. I trusted my own knowing of who I really am. It came from the natural evolution of maturity and hard-lived experiences. It also came from an epiphanic moment of realization that other people's narratives of who we are can have nothing to do with us. The process of trying to convince someone of who we really are when they are already certain that their version of us is accurate, is utterly exhausting and ultimately pointless.

If you love your husband profoundly but his insecurities tell him you could up and leave at any time, then the relationship gets stuck in an endless Möbius strip of oppositional beliefs: me believing that my meticulous execution of daily responsibilities is enough to register my undying commitment, Jesse believing these tasks undertaken are nothing more than the pedestrian fulfilment of being a wife and mother.

When I eventually refused to play the role he had assigned for me, I was also letting go a life-long anvil I had created for myself. I had allowed the men in my life to define me, which is so incredibly cliché to say. But I had operated in a people-pleasing cloud of over-sensitivity for too many years. To every man I thought I needed approval from, I had given permission to write an indelible description of me. I had made decisions from the broken perspective of a misunderstood, highly sensitive child, always clawing for scraps of praise from those most unlikely to give it. It was my dysfunctional habit, my default wiring, and it needed disrupting before it strangled all possibility of a healthy relationship.

I'm not sure exactly when it happened, this epiphany, but it marched in like Joan of Arc and woke me up with a fury. I saw myself in all my flaws and shortcomings and offered up an olive branch of tolerance and self-compassion.

I began a relentless campaign of radical self-acceptance. I failed often; I still fail. But I felt how this new acceptance was softening my hard edges. I realized that self-acceptance was the opposite side of the same coin as universal acceptance, in other words, the more fully I came to accept myself, the more capable I was of accepting others. I adjusted my inner thoughts like they were sound waves that needed fine-tuning. I honed them bit by bit through all the static, and smoothed them over with deliberate and soothing words. Subduing an inner critic takes constant, mindful effort, but those scattered glimpses of peace eventually stuck in my psyche.

When we make these inner shifts, I believe it's like sending a siren out into the universe. A celestial alarm bell that signals all things that will not fit with our new reality to come into focus for evaluation. And here I was, facing a reckoning of epic proportions. I stepped into my rage and prepared for the next explosion. Which came by way of a phone call from a duty officer at the courthouse.

"We're not sure when the judge will see him and read the charges, but can you come to the courthouse?" The duty officer had a kindly tone and I was thankful to be spoken to without admonishment. "Also, your husband is asking if you could bring him shoes and a sweater?"

This request did not evoke sympathy. My rage was sitting in my chest like an untamed tiger. I was angry at all the times he had been drunk and I had watched Dr Jekyll become Mr Hyde, mysteriously cruel and focused on making me his victim. He would transform from the kind and loving gentle man I knew into a twisted, sinister and angry character. We had fought about that too. His drunken anger. His lack of remorse, his need to blame me, to make me the reason for his rage. It was a point of contention that had our marriage holding on by a thread.

Younger me would have rushed to the courthouse, supplies in hand. I wouldn't have handed them over with a loving kiss and a "There, there, it'll be ok."

I would've resentfully dropped them at his feet. In my twenties and thirties I would have done what I perceived to be the right thing: show up for your husband when he needed support. But I would have done so out of a sense of duty, not love. I hadn't yet had the experiences that would allow me to care less about the optics of a situation and more about what was right for me. I didn't have the confidence or self-worth to put my proverbial foot down and say, "Fuck you, you can get your own ass out of jail." In my forties I was much more inclined to lean into the "Fuck you" option.

Chapter 3

YOGA PANTS

This new landscape I was charting had some familiar markers: A man I loved behaving badly, irresponsibly, recklessly. A man who couldn't look inwards at his demons so instead acted out.

I had been here before. My previous marriage had its own catastrophic and dramatic moment. A turning point so sharp and severe it had forever marred the otherwise gentle, winding scenic path that had been my late twenties.

I had just started my new career as a fashion stylist and had signed with an agent to represent me. It was a pivotal moment, and getting signed was an accomplishment I was proud of. The first big job they secured for me I was tasked with finding beautiful upscale clothing for a series of splashy advertising campaigns. I was excited and terrified. I wanted to be impressive, to let them know I was a solid bet. I wanted them to know I would do whatever it took to deliver beyond everyone's expectations. I wanted their approval.

Some of the more expensive items I would shoot a picture of and run the images to the studio for the go-ahead. To do this, I needed Polaroid film. The film was ten dollars a packet. I handed the cashier at my local grocery store a platinum visa for this small purchase.

"Sorry," she said flatly. "It's declined."

Once the embarrassment of the announcement flushed through me, I gathered my wits, "Oh. Okay, try this one." I handed her a platinum MasterCard.

"No, I'm sorry, this one is declined too."

I fumbled and muttered and apologized and gave her the last card in the deck, a platinum Amex. It has virtually no limit. I thought this will be fine. But my heart had already begun to hammer so loudly I thought everyone in the store could hear it. That dizzy lightheaded feeling had begun to hijack my nervous system.

"No. Sorry. Umm, I can't give you this one back — the system is telling me to destroy this card." She took out a pair of scissors and sliced it in two.

Panic overwhelmed me. I dug frantically around for my cell phone. I needed to call my husband. Through clenched teeth I hissed at him, "All our cards were declined and I just had to relinquish the Amex. What the hell is going on?!"

"I'm just consolidating some accounts. Use your bank card."

Something was wildly incongruent about his tone of voice and the seriousness of the moment. Everyone has a bullshit meter and despite my naive and gullible nature, mine was spinning like a whirling dervish. It was glaringly obvious he was lying. I hung up.

I left the store and, with shaking hands and hammering heart. I called him back from the cocoon of my car.

"You're lying to me. I know you're lying to me. Now tell me, WHAT THE FUCK IS GOING ON?!" I was practically shrieking and trying not to be swallowed whole by the mounting rage that was surging through me.

The moment between the question and the answer felt like the strange interminable moments before a car crash. His voice cracked and I knew I was about to get the truth. The rock-hard hammering truth that would shatter my privileged bubble of existence.

"I gambled," he said. "I'm sorry. I gambled online."

His words hit me like shrapnel and I wanted to run from the barrage that would follow.

"How much?!"

Silence.

"A hundred … a hundred and eighty … a hundred and eighty thousand."

A rapid-fire round of questions and answers were entangled in my hysteria. Eventually I hung up and called a girlfriend who lived close by.

She sat with me in my car in the parking lot of the grocery store. Inside the cabin of my car the news was shredding me alive. She found me in the wreckage, battered and broken, and tried her best to piece me back together. She offered up her credit card so I could get my job done and decided it would be best if she came with me. She was my saving grace, and I will always be grateful for her stabilizing presence that day.

All those privileged credit cards, I was a secondary card holder on them. I had no legal rights over them, no control over their limits, or their spending. I hadn't yet earned those cards; my husband had. He was a whizz with money and math and I had gladly abdicated our financial responsibilities to him. He was smart and steady and reliable and hard-working. I had felt safe and grateful for the way he operated in the world. He was the soothing, sensible antidote to my moody, creative intensity.

But a few years into our marriage he was behaving in ways I couldn't make sense of. Once, I had walked into our home office to find him sweating profusely and pacing. He had heard my footsteps on the stairs and slammed his laptop closed before I could see what he was doing. It was obvious he was trying to hide something. I knew that confronting him would have been pointless. Like a dense heavy fog his lying would drift from his lips, attempting to cover some dramatic situation. Situations he would manufacture yet never seem to recognise his role in. The complexity of the lies had become a full-time occupation for him, partly out of necessity to maintain his latest façade and partly, I believed, for his entertainment. Confronting him meant applying an effort too grand to muster. But words were unnecessary anyway. The way he was moving about the office mimicked a fly freshly caught in a spider's web, erratic and unsure whether to thrash about or succumb to the shock. He was sweating and taking shallow breaths, stuffing his clenched fists into his pockets, unable to make eye contact.

I was piecing together scenes from the last few months and a pit was growing in my stomach.

We had been to Las Vegas a few months before and he had spent the whole night at a craps table, betting five thousand dollars a hand. The table had been sectioned off with red velvet rope and he was assigned his own team of dealers and pit boss. When I asked to have a word with him I had to pass security. The scene had felt surreal, a charade that had been going on for hours. I begged him to come with me, to spend time with me, with our friends, how long was he going to play? But he was embroiled in the moment, high on adrenaline and basking in the attention. He handed me five hundred dollars and said with a jeer, "Here, go buy yourself something frilly."

The pit boss asked him as I left, "How much did you pay for her?"

The weeks and months after our financial crisis were the toughest I'd lived as an adult. I was 29 years old and completely unequipped to handle an upheaval of that magnitude. The money was the easy part to recover from. It was the lies and the gaslighting that unfolded in the aftermath that had decimated me.

He needed to frame me. I would become his scapegoat because his own behaviour had become so unconscionable he couldn't look at it. He couldn't hold himself responsible. I was at fault and he would ensure everyone in our inner circle believed it.

Addictions are complicated, very complicated. The addict is most often a broken soul who needs compassionate help, not condemnation and punishment. Somehow, gamblers seem to fall outside of that category. Their addiction seems wilful, as if they are deliberately choosing to destroy their lives and those entangled with them. But research would tell a different story. Gamblers are a different kind of addict not because of deliberate choice, but because the wiring in their brains literally bypasses the circuit that tells them they should stop.

Their adrenaline takes control and it becomes their drug of choice.

The other thing about addicts is if you corner them before they are ready to release their addiction they will fight like a rabid animal, leaving unsuspecting victims in their wake. They hurl blame and accusations around like heat-seeking missiles; the closest target will get destroyed. I found myself on the receiving end of a tactical smear campaign the scale of an American presidential election. It was my fault he needed to gamble, I was insatiable in my need for material things, he had to provide, he was under immense pressure and I wasn't pulling my weight. I was messing around trying to "find myself" while he toiled at a job that was high stress and long hours so I could sit on the couch and eat bonbons all day. He had used that phrase numerous times and I was always insulted; I didn't enjoy sitting around and I have never really liked bonbons.

In the final chapter of his narrative, I was accused by one of his family members of "riding on his coattails." I was devastated by the accusation. My friendships began to fall apart. I slowly became a pariah in his family and my creditably in certain work circles began to crumble. I felt like I was drowning in a sea of endless accusations and when I protested it would just prove that I was the shrieking lunatic of a wife he was painting me to be.

It was true that two years before I had quit my steady job to figure out what I wanted to do, and it was true that my financial contribution had been pathetic, and it was true that he worked long hours and had a high stress load. It was also true that when we first met, I was the main breadwinner. It was also true that I had willingly given everything I had to support him in his fledgling career.

That had never mattered to me. He was now doing the same for me, so I thought. So he had told me. But what he told me wasn't what he was telling the world once I discovered his addiction.

My closest relationships were eventually tattered beyond recognition. I was in distress so much of the time and most friendships can't tolerate that kind of strain. I wasn't sleeping. I was barely functional during my waking hours. Just to be in the presence of a person who is on the brink of coming undone takes tremendous patience and deep compassion. It's also unsustainable. He was broken, I was broken and ultimately our relationship survived another four years before he moved on with another woman.

In a peculiar form of kismet, many years after he had remarried, his wife and I became friends. We had mutual friendships and would find ourselves at the same social functions on occasion. One night in a bar, whilst celebrating a friend's birthday, she found herself in a margarita-fuelled confession and blurted out, "You're NOTHING like what he told me about you."

It was a pivotal moment that opened the door to several conversations over the years. I learned that she had hated me even though we had never met. I was the evil, uncaring ex who had been the reason for her husband's tortured existence. I was selfish and materialistic. My temper was epic and my fuse dangerously short. I was the character he needed me to be and it was easy — actually, required — for her to buy into his characterization. She was the adulterer after all, and their affair was easy to justify with me as the venomous, abusive wife.

Once, in a bizarre encounter at a yoga conference, with thousands of people milling about, we ran into each other in the ladies' room. Aghast at the coincidence, we laughed and wondered if this was a moment that was meant to be. There was an open-hearted exchange where we allowed ourselves simply to witness each other with humanity and without the outside interference of someone else's agenda-fuelled opinion. She had apologized for believing his lies, I told her that I knew she was a victim of his charming deceit, exactly as I had been. It was an immensely healing moment for us both.

We found ourselves at various events over the ensuing years and unfolded the secrets and lies we had been told by our master puppeteer. Lies that made our mouths gape open like watching a car crash and lies that made us laugh until we cried because of their absurdity. Our bond was sealed when ten years into their marriage she discovered that he had gambled them into a six-figure debt. He had tried to deny it, cover his tracks and then, predictably, used her as his scapegoat, claiming she was unhinged and almost succeeding in getting her committed to a mental health facility.

The stories we tell are powerful and often dangerous in the hands of an unscrupulous author. It was being the main character of another devastating narrative that had given rise to the need to surrender to my current situation. This time I would handle things differently. This time I would fight with my surrender. I would leave him to whatever story he needed to tell but stay detached and stand in the middle of the hurricane with a clear sense of my flawed, imperfect self. I was not going to be blown open again and would not let this story define the second half of my life.

Chapter 4

THE SWEATER

The duty officer was so polite I felt the tug of wanting to please him, to fulfil his request, to drop everything and do as I was asked.

"So, can you get here?" he asked me again.

"No. I can't," I said calmly. Joan of Arc was back in my head. "I have a young child and no one to leave her with. Sorry, he'll have to figure it out."

I was done being put through the wringer. I was done picking up the pieces.

Some years before I had adopted a "natural consequences" relationship style. In other words, if your kid forgets to pack their indoor shoes and has to wear their boots all day, let them. Don't run to fix it. Let them feel a little discomfort so they'll remember next time. Or, if your husband gets himself locked up and is uncomfortable, let him be uncomfortable. Let him feel the consequences.

I didn't adopt this style overnight, and it was in direct opposition to being a "good wife" and a "good mother". It took me a long time and some significant struggle to step into that role and out of the people-pleasing, accommodating, helpful, "good" human I had been trained to be.

I learned during the course of that call that Jesse was being detained on two counts of assault and one count of mischief. There's no playbook for hearing that kind of news. There's no one you can call, no helpline, no support group. The call from the duty officer had picked me up and shaken me so violently I needed to vomit again.

When I made that decision not to go to the courthouse, I knew I had made the right choice. I was angry, so very angry. I hadn't slept. I had been worried sick (literally), and then I was expected to pack up our kid, tell her god knows what untruth, and drive downtown, to help him feel more comfortable, to get him out of the chaos he had created?

"No" said Joan of Arc. "No, no, NO."

Enough was enough.

I moved about our loft, oscillating between the energy of an unstoppable raging tornado and a wounded sparrow. At one moment fuelled by the rage of years of being caught in the crosshairs of outrageous, violent, masculine behaviour and in another moment wanting to collapse from the crushing weight of this latest devastation.

My mind and body bargained relentlessly with each other for the next few hours: "Just make lunch, then you can cry." "First get outside, then you can come home and fall apart." I told Everleigh that "Daddy would be calling to explain everything" and that I really wasn't sure where he was. She has the perception of Rumi and her laser-sharp insight would not be fobbed off with some Disney-fied version of events. But I refused to be the one to have to explain what he had done; I did not want to be that storyteller. It wasn't my story, it wasn't my bullshit and it wasn't fair! I told her enough to placate her, reverting back to the parenting tactics required with toddlers, manipulating them into distraction and offering up any diversion I could.

At 3 p.m. the phone rang again. It was the same duty officer. "We're not sure if his case will be read to the court today which means they might have to detain him until Monday morning when they resume. Unless you can get here in forty-five minutes to post bond, then it's more likely they'll let him go today."

"Monday morning?" I tried not to let the panic be heard in my voice. My wheels were spinning. He had to go to work. How would he explain himself if he couldn't show up at 9 a.m.?

He'd been at this job for six months and was one of their sales superstars. He loved the job and his boss. He'd waited years to feel this kind of satisfaction. He was in an upper management role and enjoying all the perks that came with his hard work and title. We had family benefits for the first time in ten years, a luxury our self-employed status had never allowed. We had some stability and security and could finally take a breather from our decade-long freelancing roller coaster.

Another tsunami of panic washed over me, and I told the officer I'd be there. My brain was a mass of misfiring electrical circuits. It was Saturday afternoon in a city of three million people. I wouldn't drive — it would take too long. There would be no parking. I wasn't even sure where the courthouse was. I didn't have an address. Our daughter — what would I do with Everleigh? Drag her to the courthouse? No, no, leave her with a neighbour, run to the neighbour's loft, call an Uber, grab Jesse some shoes and a sweater, find the address, hurry up, hurry up! I needed to puke again.

As things turned out, there were no neighbours home that afternoon and my Uber app wouldn't accept my new credit card. I felt my nervous system screaming under the strain of the petty and not-so-petty inconveniences. I couldn't take it anymore.

I was pushing Everleigh into her coat. "Mommy you're scaring me, why are you crying? Why are you so stressed out?"

"I'm sorry honey, I'm trying to get us downtown. We have to get downtown and time is running out and I can't get us a ride."

I decided to call Clara, my friend and neighbour who would know exactly what I needed to do next. She was in the car with her husband and two little kids. I couldn't contain the panic in my voice. She was calm and fast to figure out what I needed. She called me an Uber from her phone. "It's almost there," she told me. "Just a couple more minutes."

As if she was a 911 dispatcher talking me down off a ledge. Which she pretty much was.

We headed out the door into the waiting car. Everleigh was shaking. She wanted to know what was happening. I wasn't going to break the news to her in any detail, so I told her simply, "Daddy made some very poor choices that caused a lot of trouble and he hurt some people very badly. He's going to explain it to you, ok? I'm sorry, this is scary and I'm scared too. It's going to be okay," I lied. "It's going to be okay."

Chapter 5

CHEAP SHOES

We arrived at the courthouse with twenty minutes to spare. On the ride downtown I was able to send some frantic messages to Kyle, my friend and neighbour and the father of Everleigh's best friend. He was driving back into town and would pick Everleigh up on his way home. He would take her and his own daughter, Marlowe, to go and play some games at the arcade. It would take Everleigh's mind off things and lighten the mood.

Kyle and I were both parents with no immediate family around and we had parented in our own micro-village since our girls were three years old. We always had each other's back when it came to the kids. We had both been through some domestic bedlam and we knew things about each other's marriages that only neighbours can know. We held sacred the dark truths we knew the other had confronted and consequently there was an inviolable bond between our families.

At the front of the old courthouse I passed the metal detectors and three security officers and felt for a second like I was in a scene from Law and Order. The ridiculousness of the moment landed on me like a hail of shattered glass. This couldn't possibly be real? How could I have ended up in this scene, this absurd and terrifying chapter that was getting harder and harder to erase?

Once I had passed the security checkpoint I was in the grand main lobby. The building smelled of old wood and bad ventilation. She was a majestic old architectural beauty in stunning red brick, with wide open hallways and soaring ceilings, but her grubby walls and multiple layers of paint on every doorway told a story not of epic majestic tales, but rather sordid short narratives of broken lives. Generations of bedraggled souls had drifted through these passageways.

To be standing within the bricks of this place was like taking an immersive psychic voyage into waves of sorrow, rage, uneasiness and regret. The dark little chapters were left here hanging in the air and haunting the atmosphere. I could feel the collective weight of momentary lapses in reason, of snap decisions and gross misjudgements. They were all here with me in a dense foreboding energy perched in the hand-wringing no-man's-land between accused and sentenced. These hallways had seen it all: the criminal, the deranged, the unhinged, the woeful, the angry, the hurt. And the families. The wives and the children, the parents and the siblings, trailing behind in the wreckage of the accused, white knuckled, heads pounding, throats dry. Shock gnawing at every fibre, emotional overwhelm burning through their psyches like a fireball.

We were ushered into the court, where charges were being read aloud and the parade of that day's perpetrators stood behind a glassed-in box beside the public viewing benches. A female judge sat at the top of the room listening to the offences and deciding whether the person in question should be remanded in custody or released on bond.

I sat with Everleigh beside me on an uncomfortable wooden pew and tried to will Kyle into appearing before she had to see her daddy behind that glass and listen to the charges being levied at him. The rushing noise in my ears was unbearable, my heart felt like it was going to jackhammer itself into my mouth. A police officer tapped me gently on the arm. She smiled politely and asked, "Are you here for Jesse Benton?"

I wanted to fall into her arms and sob. It was the first kindness I had felt in the madness of those hours. I could barely squeak out my answer. "Yes."

She asked me to follow her and then handed us over to a blond-haired woman wearing an innocuous grey suit, grappling with a stack of brown and manila files.

"Hi," she said. "I'm Grace. I'm one of the lawyers here. Umm, this is your daughter, yes?"

"Yes, she is," I replied.

"Okay. Perhaps she could wait in the hallway while we talk in my office? You'll be able to see her. I'll leave the door open."

I settled Everleigh onto the hallway bench with my phone for entertainment and to muffle the conversation I was about to have. I walked into the dishevelled little office adjacent to the bench and sat in a metal-framed chair, the type that belonged in a cheap hotel conference room. From the opposite side of the humble little desk, Grace opened an unlabelled file.

"I'm going to read you the charges against your husband. I assume you've already been briefed?"

Briefed? I thought, by whom? I had hearsay and scraps of information from neighbours and police officers. My heart, I was sure, was about to erupt out of my chest. "Actually, I don't know any details."

She looked at me sympathetically and I thought I might pass out. She began to read the list of charges.

"Assault," she said. Not the type of bar-brawling Saturday night drunk in an alleyway kind of assault. Assault of a woman. A woman?! And also, a firefighter. An innocent passerby and a guy just doing his job, a heroic job at that.

Jesse had targeted a pretty, petite woman who was making her way to visit friends in our building. He had picked her up and shaken her violently, thrown her against the brick wall and ripped out a chunk of her hair.

I couldn't quell the nausea. "Assault." The word hung over me like a guillotine. I could feel myself spinning into a hellish kaleidoscope of rage, shame, fear, sadness, grief, even hatred. He was about to get the wife he had made me in his mind's stage play, in his narrative, in his storyline. Jesse had finally succeeded. I hated him. I couldn't imagine what that poor woman must have felt. I couldn't imagine being thrown about like a rag doll by a man who was almost a foot taller and a hundred pounds heavier. I raged for her and for me in that moment.

Grace would read a few more lines of the charges and then pause, each time apologetic and glancing at me sympathetically. Thankfully, Kyle arrived in the hallway before she was done. His arrival was a welcome intermission to break the spell of the ongoing horrific details. Kyle had been in his own crisis of a similar magnitude if not similar nature. He already had the playbook, and his focus was immediately on getting Everleigh into his car and out of the courthouse. I knew she would be okay with her best friend by her side. They would have a sleepover with no questions asked and the girls would stay up late watching YouTube and eating candies in bed. I felt a twinge of relief as they headed out the door.

I was levelled by the three detailed pages of the charges. I was trying to keep the nausea at bay and not disintegrate into uncontrollable sobs. In addition to the unprovoked assault against the woman, Jesse had violently shoved a firefighter, and then he had run headlong into a moving bus in an attempt to stop it. It had taken several officers to subdue him because he was acting so violently and erratically. I listened to her describe the ways he had damaged other people's lives just a few hours earlier and I wanted to vanish. I wanted to evaporate into the air and let someone else step into this role. I wasn't cut out for this, God dammit. Why was this happening?!

Grace pushed some paperwork gingerly across the desk and explained that Jesse's chances of being released today would be fairly good if I could sign here, and she gestured to a dotted line. I signed the paperwork and we headed back into the courtroom. I sat on the wooden pew with half a dozen other people, most of them poorly dressed and slightly dishevelled. As a fashion stylist, I had pondered the expression of clothing thousands of times. Clothing was a great divider, immediately differentiating between the "haves" and the "have nots", a flashing billboard declaring our economic status to the world. Our clothes are also the first and most obvious message to the world of our character, our level of confidence or creativity. Given my occupation, people had often expressed some anxiety that I would judge them for their clothing choices, but the very opposite was true, I had opinions, of course, but not judgements. I knew what it felt like to be mercilessly evaluated by your clothing and I knew what it was like only to be able to afford clothes from a thrift store.

Behind me was a sketch artist, quietly and precisely scratching out the faces of the perpetrators and the court employees. I froze with the thought that Jesse's face could end up in lines of coloured pencil on the pages of a newspaper. His charges were pretty sensational, and his story could've made an enticing headline. We had been in the national papers before, but for feel-good lifestyle stories, or as a consequence of my work. I hoped the artist wouldn't have time to sketch him accurately. I hoped he was tired and was losing interest; it was the end of the day after all.

I was glad that the court required people to stay silent and to sit calmly. If I had reacted to the way I was feeling inside I would have been screaming and sobbing uncontrollably.

I waited for another ten minutes or so, until Jesse was brought into the box. He was led by an officer of the court, his hands shackled in handcuffs in front of him. His face was puffy and he had a faint black eye. He had scratches up his arms and his cotton polo shirt looked like he had been sleeping in it for a week. He was behind the glass box to my left and slightly in front of me. I could observe him like a zoo animal. I felt a blend of shame and, despite my earlier sentiments, compassion.

The judge listened to the charges and was informed that I was present in the court. I didn't want her to notice me, I didn't want anyone to notice me. She addressed Jesse directly, "Mr Benton, the charges against you are extremely serious. The terror that you have caused a young woman will affect her for the rest of her life. Do you have any prior criminal charges, Mr Benton?"

A court lawyer responded, "A DUI your worship when the defendant was 18 years old."

The judge looked back at Jesse, "Do you understand the charges that are made against you, Mr Benton?"

Jesse shuffled to the small microphone in the front of the glass box. He cleared his throat. His voice was scratchy. "Yes your worship."

"I'm informed that you are ordinarily a responsible person, with a family, with no significant priors and are not a flight risk. Therefore I'm releasing you based on the court's recommendation. I hope you have some time to think about the ramifications of your actions, Mr Benton."

An officer at the front of the glass box opened the door and unlocked his handcuffs. Jesse stepped into the public space and made his way around to the bench I was seated on. He was shuffling towards me in a pair of black cotton shoes with cheap plastic soles. They clearly didn't fit. His heels were hanging off the backs — a size thirteen foot isn't easy to accommodate.

I had never thought about the fact that shoes would be something you would find in a jail. I wondered how many people were arrested who didn't have footwear. When Jesse had left our loft the night before he was wearing his shoes. Who knows how and when he had lost them? Just another casualty of the madness, I thought. It made me angrier. He was always losing and damaging clothes. The lost shoes were a symbol of his carelessness, his blatant disregard for the damage he was capable of wreaking.

We didn't speak, save for a few mumbles and gestures towards the sweater and boots I had hurriedly stuffed into a plastic bag. He couldn't get his boots on; they were Blundstones, the type that you pull-on with the help of a tab at the back. His hand was badly swollen and he couldn't grip the tab. It meant I had to help him. I didn't want to help him. I had shed my good-wife skin and I wasn't about to pretend everything was okay. Nothing about this scenario was okay. I was no longer here to help assist in the wake of mass destruction, I was no longer available for the experience of saviour and saint. Where does "good wife" end and self-preservation begin?

The Jesse I had envisioned collecting from the courthouse was remorseful and profoundly apologetic, concerned about his family and what he had put us through. The Jesse that materialized in front of me was angry. His body was badly hurt and his ordeal was evident in the way he moved about. He wasn't grateful that I had come to collect him. He didn't apologize for anything. In fact, he showed not a sliver of remorse or concern, other than for his own discomfort.

My fantasy of how he should behave evaporated and a rage began to boil inside of me. If I had so much as been caught in an illegal parking spot my regret and desire to make amends would have chewed me up until I could put things right. It wasn't that I considered myself some morally superior being, but I simply couldn't grasp Jesse's agitated, unrepentant demeanour. Perhaps this crushing realisation that he wasn't going to deliver the repentance I had anticipated was in fact an ongoing theme in all my relationships. Maybe I had fantasised my way through all kinds of disappointments, overlooking what was actually happening in favour of how I wanted it to look.

We sat mostly in silence on the twenty-minute drive back to our loft. His occasional utterance of pain fuelled my seething anger. I dared not speak; the words that would form would be the end of us. Maybe this was the end of us anyway. How could this be? How could this kind, loving, gentle, thoughtful man be so utterly unremorseful, so oblivious to the carnage he had left in his wake? How could he be so entirely self-absorbed and concerned about his own comfort? How could we, his family, "his girls", not even be on his radar right now?

We arrived at our loft and in the privacy of our own space my questions flew at him with white-hot anger.

"What the fuck did you do to that poor woman?! WHY Jesse?! I can't make sense of any of this. What the hell were you thinking? Do you have ANY idea what you put us through? I'm not telling Everleigh, that's your fucking job. You get to explain everything, I'm not doing it. I'M NOT DOING IT!"

He angrily and dismissively dodged my questions and defended himself with a statement about the judge exaggerating the charges. He reached for some Advil and began to strip off his clothes as I followed him up the stairs, still firing out questions like arrows. I trailed after him, fully armoured, wielding my sword of injustice, seething with questions that weren't getting anywhere.

Standing in our bedroom I saw the evidence of the violence that had happened hours before. The side of his torso was a mass of punctures with one spot in particular a flaming red sore about an inch in diameter.

"Oh my god …" my voice trailed off its rageful path and slid into the quiet cavern of my own pain. I was flooded with compassion, but only for a moment.

"Cops," he said. "They tased me, three fucking times."

I snapped back into my anger, my inner dialogue ranting. Of course they did, you idiot! What the fuck else were they supposed to do?

"Well, you're a big dude, they were just doing their jobs. I'm sure it wasn't easy taking down a violent lunatic."

"It was more than 'doing their jobs' — they wanted to annihilate me. Apparently one of our neighbours called 911, told them I had military training and might have a weapon. They were cops on a mission, three times they tased me, THREE times!"

And if you were dark-skinned, I thought to myself, they likely would have shot you.

"I'm going to bed. I spent the night in a freezing cold cell with a bunch of drunk guys."

I wanted to say, "Aww muffin", which were the words he would say to me to mock me if I complained unnecessarily, sometimes cheekily, sometimes with a barb attached.

My shield went back up and I knew that shutting up was the best defence. I left the room in a fury.

In the silence of the next few hours I hoped that remorse was going to land on him like the anvil Wylie Coyote always tried to drop on the Road Runner. I hoped he would notice the pain he had caused. I hoped he would notice that I was in tatters. But it never came. He outmanoeuvred any guilt, any sense of accountability, absurdly minimizing the consequences, just like a cartoon character, just like the Road Runner falling off a cliff and popping himself back up after a dramatic splat.

In the days that followed there was no remorse, no acknowledgment of the truth, no acknowledgment of anything other than his own discomfort and the charges that were "blown out of proportion". This felt familiar, his narrative, my narrative, with both of us pulling at opposite ends of a rope trying to drag each other into our own truths. But this time it felt like gaslighting. I wondered if I was on repeat, if my history of attracting shitty men was destined to loop around and around until I spun into a mania I couldn't escape. I wondered if fourteen years ago I had met a guy who had ultimately succeeded in duping me. Perhaps I was the fool; perhaps I had only seen what I wanted to see; perhaps I wasn't worthy of stable, secure relationships. Perhaps I needed to make changes. Again.

Chapter 6

SUITS

Jesse crammed his swollen body into his work clothes on Monday morning.

"You're sure?" I said. "You're sure you should tell Pete?"

Pete was his boss, a guy he trusted and respected. They had a natural and easy-going rapport and a mutual appreciation of each other.

"Yeah," he answered. "I have to come clean. Look at me. Kinda hard to say I had a great weekend."

"But this happened on a Friday night. It's none of their business," I countered.

"Nope. I can't hide it. It wouldn't feel right."¬¬

I at least respected his honesty and integrity for his job.

Around 11 a.m. he called me.

"I'm coming home."

My heart lurched in its battered cavity. I was afraid to ask the obvious.

"I went into Pete's office and he was already waiting for me with a piece of paper in his hand from HR. Apparently someone from our neighbourhood works in the legal department here and took a video of me while I was getting arrested."

Jesus! What were the chances of being unknowingly filmed on the worst day of your life by a work colleague you'd never met?!

"You can't see my face, but you hear my name," Jesse continued, "When the cops were tasing me there was this guy standing off to the side. He was yelling at me, asking my name. You can hear me yelling back on the video. Now that I think about it, it was weird this guy took such an interest in knowing who I was. I guess he had an idea that he'd seen me around the office. There must've been something familiar about me. Anyway, this guy already sent Pete the video late Friday night. So by the time I walked into his office this morning, he already knew everything that went down. Mike was in there too, you know, VP Mike, he's given me the name of a good lawyer, he thinks I'll need one since I've got criminal charges. Yeah, so anyway, they want me to take a few days off, let the dust settle a bit."

He was still treating this like it would blow over, like somehow the woman he attacked would forgive and forget, move on with her life. Like I would resume life as normal: wife, mother, hit play, repeat. The magnitude hadn't even reached him yet, let alone shaken him. I wondered if he was having some kind of delayed shock response. I wondered if I was being too dramatic. I wondered if I was losing my grip on reality.

Jesse arrived home and made a call to the lawyer that Mike had given him the number for.

"Daniel?"

"Speaking."

"Yeah, umm, Mike Carson recommended I give you a call."

"Yes, actually he already called me, you're Jesse right? Benton, is it?"

They exchanged details of what had happened. Every word was like a paper cut, an absurdly sharp pain. I could barely stay in the room as the horror was projected back onto my inner screen. I had to get it together, I had to find some kind of relief. The intensity of the last few days was unbearable. I tried another train of thought. At least this guy Daniel sounded like he was the right guy. At least Jesse knew people, people who would have clear heads and the right connections and experience to navigate the legal terrain we were about to negotiate.

"Okay," said Jesse, "I'll get you the documents right away. Is a credit card okay for your retainer?"

"Ten thousand dollars plus taxes" was the next gut-punch. I had just drained my life savings a few weeks earlier to cover other expenses. My once high-flying career had been stalling out for too long. I couldn't seem to figure out how to pivot my life's work, which paid well, into something that delivered a regular paycheque. So in a last-ditch attempt before we would have to make a more drastic move, I had withdrawn my retirement savings. We simply couldn't take another financial hit. The nausea careened through me again. I wanted to tap out, to scream at the universe, "I'M DONE! I CAN'T TAKE ANYMORE! SOMEONE PLEASE TAKE OVER MY SHIT-SHOW OF A LIFE!"

The money spewed out of my account and into the coffers labelled "defence fund". I screamed silently in the shower, hoping it would allow some of my rage to escape. Maybe this ten-thousand-dollar price tag would force him to recognize the impact of his actions, the seriousness of the situation. Maybe now he'd actually start to feel bad. Or maybe I should stop hoping that he would be different and focus on my next move.

I had been caught in the hurricane of a man's bad behaviour one too many times and I needed to get back into my Joan of Arc energy. I needed to take care of Everleigh and support her on my own if I had to. God knows, her dad could be in jail in a few months. I needed to do something. I needed a plan. Something bulletproof, something that would never allow me to be in this type of madness ever again.

Chapter 7

T-SHIRT

Until the age of twenty-eight I worked in a small business that sold a variety of products to the film industry. It had been a phenomenal introduction to entrepreneurship, as the small operation required us to wear a wide variety of hats. But I had reached as far as I could go within the business and wanted to explore a more creative path. In a leap of faith and armed with every career book I could devour, I quit my job and spent almost two years trying to find my path. I eventually landed on being a stylist, which satisfied my need for creative expression and constant variety. But what had once been a perfect fit now felt like an uncomfortable pair of old shoes.

I was a middle-aged woman with an ailing career — one that I had once prioritized over everything but now no longer supported us, and after twenty-three years I had no love left for it. It didn't challenge me or satisfy me. I adored my small circle of clients and relished the days I could be with them on set. But I was now considered too old for the youth-obsessed profession. And that obsession with youth did not just pertain to the actors and models in front of the camera, but also for those who brought the elements of beauty and style as stylists, makeup artists, art directors and photographers. We had an obligation to know and understand the latest trends, but our industry would often treat that knowledge as if it belonged exclusively to the youngest generation. I had once heard a crew member speaking about a fellow stylist as "over the hill", saying they had "just lost it". As if beauty, style and relevance within a culture had a sell-by date.

Although I loved my work, I had struggled for years with the contradiction of participating in an industry whose subtext was always that women were not enough, therefore will buy more shit they don't need. Neither was I comfortable with the destructive and absurd notion that conforming to impossible standards of beauty was the path to acceptance. I had longed for more inclusive representation in ad campaigns and more body-positive messages in magazines, but would be met with a polite smile and a suggestion that what people really wanted to see was "aspirational" not "real life". I was tired of the carbon-copy ad briefs describing pretty white girls doing wholesome, domestic things in perfectly pressed outfits, in palatial, impeccable homes with their two blond children smiling happily at their feet.

For years I felt as if I was sitting on the sidelines waving a red flag that the industry was going to go up in flames if we didn't start making changes. If we didn't start telling stories that made people more-than, not less-than. If we didn't start representing beauty beyond the tokenism of a brown girl, black girl and Asian girl, attempting to make ourselves feel better for being so inclusive.

I had been so outraged by it all that in 2011, I had run a series of workshops to help women make easy style choices, but it was really a cover for trying to boost our collective crappy self-esteem. The series had garnered the attention of one of our national newspapers and ended up on the front page of the style section. This had helped to fill my need for making meaning out of a frivolous occupation and eased my guilt for participating in the lies we told.

My career had afforded me the privilege of working with a myriad of celebrities, appearing on dozens of television shows and travelling to incredible places, and it had been spectacular. But it would not feed my soul, and there were too many aspects of it that made me angry: how elitist and narrow-minded a supposedly wildly creative industry actually was, at least within the confines of the conservative Canadian culture. I had no time for its pretentious nature, or cliquey, impenetrable tribes.

Canada had been my home since I was nineteen years old, and it had always felt more like home than my native UK. I loved the positivity of the place, the can-do attitude and friendly nature of its people. I had rented my first apartment in Toronto when I was twenty-one; the city had raised me and grown around me into almost three million strong. The financial titan of Canada, it lacked the ferocious colourful creativity and loud-mouthed flavour of New York and didn't have the confidence and culture of London, but it was young and optimistic, learning to grow into its identity. I felt privileged to bear witness to its coming of age, and to have enjoyed a successful career with plenty of splashy appearances on national TV and in some glossy magazines.

But I had earned the "been there, done that" T-shirt, and the city was no longer a reflection of who I had become. It had become overcrowded, like every large metropolis, its shiny streets crammed with overpriced, insipid glass-block condo towers. Hipsters began dominating the cultural scene, creating a demand for artsy bars and cafes peddling twelve-dollar avocado toast by day and twenty-dollar cocktails by night. Driving through town was like playing a high-risk video game, an assault on the senses that left the most capable drivers an octave more on edge. Public transit rides were a test of tolerance, bashed by backpacks, or stepped-on toes in crowded subway cars and my personal favourite, the offensive summertime odour of those who did not wear deodorant. The city and I had outgrown each other. I had become quieter, calmer and more reflective, while the city had become louder and jostled with a high-speed competitive energy. I was worn out by it, and I needed to move on.

It wasn't just the physical environment of Toronto that I was tired of, it was trying to be myself within the restrictions of such a conservative culture. I had landed myself in plenty of hot water by boisterously expressing my opinions. Several Canadians had said to me, "Why don't you tell us how you really feel?" delivered with sarcastic outrage. It had always baffled me — why wouldn't I tell someone how I really felt? It seemed bizarre to pretend I felt something I didn't. Even after twenty-seven years of love for this country, I couldn't understand this Canadian proclivity to tell people what they wanted to hear.

The compulsive politeness that permeated everything was delightful and charming until I became more interested in being myself and less concerned with pleasing anyone else. These small and peculiar Canadian-isms that made people agree to coming for dinner when they actually had no intention of showing up, or the sideways remarks I'd experienced if a family member was mad at me. It had worked its way under my skin and I found the passive-aggressive tone all too pervasive and exhausting.

We grated on each other's nerves and I longed for the feisty banter I used to enjoy with friends in the UK. A few of my Canadian friendships would tolerate these types of exchanges, but they were the exception and not the rule. I felt as though my wings were clipped trying to conform to the political correctness of a country I loved but that wasn't ready to accommodate my not-so-good-girl persona. I figured it would be only a matter of time before I would offend someone to the point of no return.

Jesse was home for the next five days, either slumped on the couch or endlessly napping his way through the daylight hours. My silence was no longer knife edged. I had retreated into my own inner world and had decided to make some big moves. The shift had given me a direction, a feeling of control that I desperately needed. I decided I needed to go back to school, and I decided I needed to move back to the UK.

Jesse's family was very Canadian: kind and friendly, generous and considerate. But they were my family through marriage, and they weren't about to drive the two- or four-hour drive to check on me. They would call periodically and I could drive there, but this subtle distinction in boundaries would always have me placed at the edge of assistance, not in the centre, as my own parents would have made me. I understood that their allegiance would always be with their son/brother, no matter what he had done. I'm quite sure that in their shoes I would have made the same choice. However, the understanding that no one was going to come to my aid had made me certain that I needed to go home.

I had always wanted to complete my education and get the degree I'd originally been working towards. When I'd arrived in Canada I was a foreign student and the subsequent school fees were out of the question. I had put myself through some night courses at the local universities and colleges once I had a steady job. But I had never accomplished a degree and I hated filling out those forms that ask about your level of education and having to tick the "high-school" box. I was relentlessly driven to accomplish, succeed, prove, prove, prove. By this time I'd realized this was just another dysfunctional symptom of my need for acceptance. Perhaps if I could brag about which university I had gone to, which degree I had achieved, then people would just know that I was smart. I would be accepted into the whisky-sipping circles of academics and my opinion would matter. But that realization did not displace my desire for education. My reasons were more personal and less acceptance-seeking, but I still wanted that degree.

Having made these decisions, that week I filled out application forms to universities in the UK while Jesse napped. I had always wanted to study psychology. Perhaps I could find my soul-tribe of other screwed-up individuals with a bookcase full of self-help books and embarrassingly large therapy bills. It seemed like a blinding flash of the obvious that I would be drawn to a topic that could help me unravel the messy knots and frayed edges that had been my life. Besides, it felt like the perfect antidote to the first chapter of my career that was entirely focused on external aesthetics. I needed something with substance that could satiate my appetite for understanding.

I ploughed through the pages of application forms for Sheffield University. It had an excellent psychology department and was miraculously located within half an hour of my parent's home. My parents. What in the hell do I say to my parents?

"Hey Mum and Dad, so uh, Jesse took a bunch of magic mushrooms, had a really bad trip, assaulted a woman and a firefighter and now I hate him. Also, he could go to jail, but don't worry, I just drained my life savings so hopefully that won't happen. And! Can I come live at home while I go to Uni? Oh, and I'll bring your grandkid with me as a bonus. Cool?"

The synopsis of the last few days was no less absurd than the minute-by-minute play-by-play. I wasn't going to tell my folks. He was going to have to do it. That decision was rooted in my rebellion against playing the good wife; she was no longer available to soften the blow or play spin-doctor with family members.

Jesse slouched from bed to couch and back again. Still showing no signs of remorse, but for the first time in the fourteen years we had been together he looked depressed.

He was depressed. It finally seemed like an appropriate response. I couldn't yet access compassion for him; my own pain was too raw. If I focused on the future and what I could make it, I could get through this. If I could zoom out of my everyday life I would stand a chance of surviving.

Truthfully, I was frantic in those days after that Friday night. I was spinning at high speed and crashing into despair. Making plans for my future and filling out the application forms were ways I could temporarily stop the spinning. I would have to focus and look forward. Keep. Moving. Forward. Do. Not. Collapse.

Chapter 8

LOUNGEWEAR

Sometime in the long days that Jesse was at home, he picked up a particular book that had been perched on our desk for weeks. I had borrowed the book from a neighbour, whose brother, Daemon Fairless, had written it. Fairless was a journalist and neuroscientist. I had been idly chatting with this neighbour and we had landed on a discussion about male aggression. He confided that his brother Daemon had wrestled with aggressive tendencies and explained how it had almost destroyed his marriage. As he described his brother, I felt like he was describing Jesse. Daemon had drilled down into his own vigilante behaviour and that of violent criminals. He had discovered a link between high levels of testosterone and aggression. He had interviewed criminals in an attempt to understand their motivation, and in the process discovered his own shortcomings and exposed them in a book he titled Mad Blood Stirring.

Jesse was not a reader, save for the copies of Popular Mechanics that came in the mail every month. But he was here, stuck at home, aimless and depressed, and this book's title called to him. I sat on my laptop planning my new life, stabbing at the keyboard with a focused fury, while he slowly turned the pages, engrossed in every word, occasionally sharing a passage that had resonated. He reached for a box of Kleenex on several occasions as he wept through many of the passages. Somehow this book had woven an invisible thread between us. It had penetrated his anger and consequently had given me hope. I wanted our family to stay together, despite everything. Jesse and I had a deep connection from the moment we met, and now we not only had history but also the shared DNA in the form of a perfect little human being.

It was the following Friday morning, right after we had delivered Everleigh to school, that Jesse finally allowed the pain he was trying to suffocate a chance to breathe. We sat at the kitchen island, half-consumed cups of coffee in white ceramic mugs on a white quartz countertop. A slightly sterile scene, if it weren't for the breakfast dishes scattered and the chopping board with discarded bits of strawberries. He began to talk.

He was always economic with his words; I had had to learn to deliver my asks in short and simple sentences, which isn't to imply that he's stupid or incapable. Just the opposite, really. His military-type mind operates on bare bones information. Details are superfluous and he would glaze over if I offered too much information. So when the words began tumbling out of his mouth I knew he was about to unleash an almighty torrent of stifled emotion.

He sat in the kitchen chair with his normally squared shoulders rolled forward in defeat. He pressed his good hand into his eyes, trying to control the tears that were rushing forward. Finally, a glimmer of hope. Remorse had arrived and was slashing away at his steely nonchalance. Perhaps I hadn't been duped again by a charming, charismatic maniac after all. He sobbed, and words of understanding, born of self-reflection, gushed out of him. Daemon's book had spoken to him like some kind of biblical sermon. It had offered him insight into his own behaviour, and he was struck with epiphanies lighting from his brain as if they were fireflies being set free from a jar.

He described a scene in the book where Daemon had intervened in an aggressive altercation unfolding on the street. His wife and young child were in tow when he decided to step in and "resolve" the conflict. The moment had been a pivotal one for Daemon. His wife had later pointed out how he had put them in an impossible situation while putting his own life in danger. Hijacked by his testosterone, Daemon had been convinced his intervention was required. In his storyline he was the heroic, righteous vigilante who would need to teach these fools a lesson. Jesse had recognized himself and was finally able to look beyond his own lens and comprehend the impact of his behaviour.

Daemon's own pivotal moment became Jesse's, and his recognition became the linchpin that unlocked some compassion I had wanted to feel but hadn't been able to access through my own pain and disappointment.

I let him have the moment of despair, knowing how vital it was to simply stay present and bear witness. I knew from my own moments of collapse that the way others choose to be present around us during times such as these strongly affects the outcome. I recalled many moments sitting in my therapist's office in the safety of her big, squishy armchair and oversized pillows, my body and mind sinking into the soft support. She had witnessed hundreds of people in a kaleidoscope of emotions and when tormented patients finally unlocked their bound-up grief the most powerful presence in the room was her silence. She understood that our souls demanded it. Silence offered with reverence and respect was the ultimate panacea in the throes of untangling emotional knots. A person who will rush for Kleenex to appease their own discomfort, or a person who will leap to their feet for an awkward hug, or a person who will inappropriately attempt to distract from the pain offers all the wrong responses. I sat there quietly, allowed his heart to be seen and felt my own sliver of relief.

In the days that followed I discussed my plans to go back to school and to make a new career for myself. I was operating as I had seen every man in my life operate — taking charge of my destiny, unapologetically, unconcerned even, about the ramifications on family members. I was doing what I had to do. I was going to go home — back to England, back to the safety of my own family — and secure myself a future. A bulletproof future for Everleigh and me, that no man could destroy.

Jesse was shockingly supportive of the idea. I supposed because he had been the main breadwinner for too long in our relationship and he was worn out from the high-stress jobs and breakneck speed. I wasn't yet sure if our marriage would survive this level of stress. I wasn't sure he wasn't going to end up in jail, or with a criminal record and not be able to live outside of Canada. I didn't know if getting my degree in the UK and making a life for myself and Everleigh was going to involve him or not, but I knew I needed to be surrounded by people I loved, who loved me and would offer their unconditional support. I needed to be where there were no surprises, a place where I could bring Everleigh and relax my white-knuckled grip on life for a while.

The Skype call Jesse had with my parents went as I would have predicted. My mother gazed off into the distance and I knew she would be raging at him. Raging at how I had been put in this situation again, raging at how he could be so immature, raging for Everleigh and the sheer stupidity of his choice. My dad did what he always does: processes the emotion, gets that out the way, then organizes himself a mental spreadsheet and gets to work on the problem. He always told me it was "an engineer thing" but I suspected his brain was simply wired that way and being an engineer just happened to be the perfect reflection of who he is. During the call I divulged my hopes of going to Sheffield Uni and gingerly broached the subject of staying with them for the duration. I have been incredibly lucky to have such supportive parents, especially when it came to any kind of self-improvement and education. To my enormous relief they agreed to the plan and within a week, I had booked a solo flight to stay for ten days and lay down the tracks for my new bulletproof life.

Chapter 9

FED-EX UNIFORM

My flight was scheduled to depart on December 8th. Now I had a target to work towards and was taking the first step in my plan towards total independence. My days of operating as a "good wife" were over and I knew this would be met with some considerable judgments. I knew that some of Jesse's family would see me as selfish and unsupportive. But this was a matter of self-preservation. Living in a world where I was tossed around in the wake of reckless behaviour was causing me to oscillate in an exhausting state between hyper-vigilance and imploding despair. I had allowed myself to be in this situation not just once, but twice! I had to get some control back in my life and I had to support Everleigh. The pressure to create a stable future for us was immense, but the alternative was to do nothing and watch my existing life burn to the ground. Keep. Moving. Forward.

In the weeks before my flight, our loft was filled with equal parts sadness and anger, occasionally interrupted by an injection of gut-wrenching news. A letter arrived by Fed-Ex. Jesse signed for it and ripped open the cardboard envelope with his name on it. It was a perfectly typed letter on cream coloured paper, with a crest-type logo placed neatly at the top in the centre. At first glance I guessed it must be from the court. As he read it I could tell by his facial expression he was fighting the urge to tear it up or throw it at the wall.

My nervous system hadn't been able to calm down for days, and moments like this spiked it until nausea cascaded over me.

"What?" I asked, not really wanting to know.

"It's from The Board."

He was referring to our condo building's board of directors. He had sat in one of the three chairs for a brief period but had had a falling out with another board member when he showed up to a monthly meeting with a beer in hand. Jesse pretty much always had a beer in his hand past six o'clock. He drank the stuff like other people drink fizzy pop. He enjoyed the taste. He didn't drink it to get drunk; he just liked it and that was all there was to it as far as he was concerned. But this other board member had taken offence to his seemingly lackadaisical beer-in-hand approach and had challenged him. He told Jesse he was being disrespectful. Jesse thought the guy had become a power-mongering pedant and a whole chain of insults were exchanged. Jesse quit that night, refusing to go back to the meeting. It was a sour ending to what had once been a friendship.

This board member and his wife were people I had known since we moved in ten years ago. Our kids had played together and many a Friday night had been spent with them over pizza and play dates. I didn't want to be involved in the squabble between Jesse and this man, but the guy had texted me on occasion, suggesting I rein my husband in. Ha! As if that were even possible. I had been annoyed at the suggestion, and politely proposed that if a modification of behaviour was required that it should be addressed with the person in question, not through me. I was not responsible for Jesse's behaviour. "Not my circus, not my monkeys" was a phrase I liked to repeat to myself on too many occasions.

The letter was from the condo's law firm and was a list of by-laws that Jesse had been in violation of that fateful Friday night. One of the infractions was "loitering" in front of the building. I thought, how does one loiter in front of their own home? The list of charges ended with a threatening of further legal action, and we were to pay the legal fees associated with drafting the letter. The charges had made us both furious. It had felt like a final kick to the gut when we were already on the ground. It seemed cruel and reeked of petty vengeance.

We had suspected the letter had been spearheaded by the disgruntled board member and our suspicions were confirmed when I encountered him with his wife just outside the parking garage that week. I was on foot, walking our dog as they drove past me. Typically we would exchange a wave, a nod, a pleasantry of some kind. But that didn't happen. They were deliberately trying to ignore me and I was crushed. This tiny moment had catapulted me back to all the other moments when I had been judged and condemned because of what my husband had done. I wanted to scream, "HOW DARE YOU?! I DIDN'T DO ANYTHING WRONG!"

My anger was a thinly veiled curtain that shrouded a deep and painful sadness. This was yet another relationship that would suffer in the aftermath of a choice I didn't make.

Unfortunately, Jesse's rampage did happen on our doorstep, and plenty of neighbours had either witnessed or heard about the mayhem. Every time I was in the public spaces of our building I wondered if I was being judged or gossiped about. But it would be too easy to assume the worst of people and I wasn't about to play into my own paranoia. I didn't want to exaggerate our circumstances with fear-based allegations of my own creation. Nor was I going to slink around the building, dodging my neighbours and wearing a mantle of guilt. I had nothing to be ashamed of. Yet I felt inexplicable shame. Somehow in choosing a man who made reckless choices, I was implicated. It was wildly unfair and the injustice of all it stirred an outrage within me.

Chapter 10

BLACK PARKAS

My neighbours were good people, kind people, caring people, and the majority of them knew us well enough to withhold judgment. A few of them came to my door with offerings of cups of coffee or invitations to go for a walk. I was so grateful for their small gestures of kindness. It was a show of acceptance, of love and reassurance.

One neighbour in particular was a trauma expert, a respected voice in the recovery community and a woman who I knew would be able to help me calm my frayed nerves. I called her one morning when I couldn't get my heart to stop pounding and couldn't get the nausea to stop.

"Leyla, I was hoping you might be able to help me …" I couldn't get to the end of my sentence without breaking down. She was someone I knew would be able to hold my misery without taking it on. She would be able to hear me with compassion and suspend all judgements. She would be an iron pillar of strength and help me put aside my sword and take off my armour, if only for a few minutes. She was outside our building and invited me to join her. The simple act of walking would help regulate my nervous system.

I put on my parka, pulled my hat as far on to my head as it would go and tucked my sunglasses into my pocket. It wasn't a bright day but I wanted the ability to hide my breakdown. I wanted as many disguises as I could feasibly wear.

Our lofts were all tucked along the perimeter of the building, leaving a stunning wide open central atrium with a soaring fifty-foot ceiling, with exposed iron trusses that told the tale of its former life as a train factory. Anchored in the cavernous space below were seating pods and tiny indoor fireplaces. Our unit was on the upper level and our door opened onto a catwalk with a metal and glass railing that stretched all the way around the perimeter. From the catwalk you could see the whole space and anyone in it. It was beautiful, but exposed. More exposed than I wanted to be at that moment.

I hurried out the door with no explanation, I was preoccupied with getting out of our building and reaching Leyla without being seen. I was always stopping to chit-chat with neighbours. I enjoyed the surprise of running into people and my social nature craved these interactions. Jesse would always politely excuse himself whenever I ran into the people that had the time and energy to engage. He knew that we could banter back and forth for twenty minutes or more.

We had fought about it on occasion. He had accused me of talking too much and from his perspective, he was right. But conversation has always been one of the greatest pleasures of my life, my way to connect with the world, a fascinating and imperfect tool with a kaleidoscope of subjects waiting to be explored. The younger version of me would've bent myself into a pretzel to change my chatty ways and the comment would've wounded me immensely. But the middle-aged me had decided to acknowledge his observation rather than absorb it as an insult. If he was annoyed by the fact that I wanted to chat away the time with neighbours then he was entitled to excuse himself. And I was entitled to stay and talk. Besides, if I wasn't going to get engaging conversation from my spouse then I would get it where I could take it. It was a necessary ingredient of the stew that kept me healthy and happy.

On this occasion I wished I wasn't the social butterfly the building residents knew me to be. I really didn't want to run into anyone. I knew I would struggle to exchange pleasantries. I wore my heart on my sleeve, sometimes with too much intensity. I had passion that could easily be construed as drama in my younger years and I certainly didn't want to be perceived as a drama queen now. I had learned from my previous disaster in dealing with the aftermath of a gambling addiction that people don't really want to get too close to the problem. As I had learned during the gambling crisis in my former marriage, people in crisis are intense; they aren't easy for the average Joe to handle. It takes patience and an immense amount of understanding. Most people are simply not equipped to deal with the fallout.

Luckily, it was mid-morning, after the commuters had left the building. The catwalk was quiet and the atrium below deserted. I hurried past doorways in the hopes I wouldn't be discovered. I reached the stairwell with its white concrete walls and black iron railing. The space echoed thunderously into the high ceiling and my footsteps sounded deafening. I scurried down the three flights of stairs and into the brightly lit passageway with its tall mullioned industrial windows. A few more paces and I'd be on the side street at the back of our building, tucked away from the friendly neighbours I couldn't face.

Leyla was crossing the driveway entrance into the back of our building. We were both bundled in our long black puffy parkas, the uniform of choice for urban-dwelling Torontonians. November wasn't the worst of the Canadian winter months, but it could have a biting chill that was the precursor for what was to come. She kept a steady pace towards me and when she saw my face her eyes filled with kindness. She gently asked if I had had a hug from anyone in the last week. The simplicity and thoughtfulness of her question took me to my knees. My eyes welled up and she asked if I would like one. I nodded. I couldn't access any words for once.

She wrapped me up in her arms. We stood there for at least a minute, in view of anyone sipping their latte in the coffee shop across the street. For a moment I let myself collapse. She was propping me up with her knowing and her steady, sinewy frame.

I realized that with her small gesture she had taken off the crushing weight I had been trying to shoulder and it accentuated how little support I had around me. Somehow people who have walked through the flames of their own trauma can see the raging fire in others and have a depth of compassion and knowing that only experience can yield.

Once Leyla released me from her ballerina-like arms she steadied my shoulders and aimed her laser-like gaze right into my eyes. It was another tiny motion that made me feel seen and cared for, acknowledged and understood. It was something of a holy moment, unfolding unceremoniously in front of the coffee shop.

"Would you like to walk?" she asked gently. "It will help to regulate your nervous system, which I imagine has been working overtime."

I nodded my head and we began a slow-paced meander around the neighbourhood. Leyla had heard about the incident. The cacophony of sirens had been blaring right outside her door and later that weekend neighbours had given her their account of the drama. But Leyla wasn't inclined to gossip and her non-judgmental nature was the result of soulful wisdom, keen intuition and her vast understanding of human behaviour, particularly when under extreme stress.

For most of the walk she thoughtfully offered me simple choices, "Would you like to cross here?" or, "Would you like to rest for a minute?"

Her tone was steady and tender and very few words were actually exchanged. There were no probing questions or awkward lines of inquiry, just a few well-chosen words that helped me feel a little repaired.

The second week after what we had come to refer to as "the incident", Jesse had still received no word about his work. Without his job to go to every day, he slept even more. His depression became darker and more worrisome. Some days we both found it hard to get out of bed. The air in our loft was stagnant.

Every object seemed too heavy; every light seemed too dim. The life force was slowly seeping out through the walls and if it wasn't for Everleigh, we may both have just given up completely.

I consoled myself and tempered my anger with the knowledge that depression is like a chamber we must visit for significant change to occur. It's the playhouse of major reckonings. I needed Jesse to come face to face with his demons for our marriage and our family to survive. I needed him to dismantle his story of how I didn't love him as much as he loved me. I needed him to examine his denial of Mr Hyde and acknowledge the destruction left in the wake of his visits. I knew that the only passage to evolution would be the murky, dark and intensely difficult journey through depression. I had to dig deep to find the faith that this was all happening for a reason. It had to have a purpose; our survival depended on it.

We moved about as though we were mired in quicksand. The hammering pace of constant anxiety was taking its toll on me. I felt worn down. I had to keep zooming out of the everyday and looking forward. I had a week to go before my flight. I hadn't asked Jesse for permission to leave as I would have done before the incident. I hadn't put anything in place for him to manage Everleigh on his own, no lists of lunches or dinner ideas, no play dates organised or after-school activities lined up. I was operating in emergency mode. I had no energy for anything beyond what was required of me moment to moment, and I had no desire to make his life more manageable while I was away. He would have to figure it out, like I always had to figure it out whenever Mr Hyde decided to make an appearance.

Chapter 11

WETSUITS

The memories of all the previous injustices had kept cropping up over the weeks we were locked up together in our loft. What the hell was wrong with me? Why couldn't I just let this stuff go? Why couldn't I just get over it? I'd never been one to hold a grudge and I was never motivated by seeking vengeance. I wanted to move on and I wanted to release these painful memories into the ether, but they wouldn't go. They haunted me and they were especially persistent in those dark days. I supposed they tapped into the unresolved anger I was feeling. They were like magnetic shards moving at speed towards my feelings of outrage and injustice.

One incident in particular kept replaying like a bad record. It had happened while we were on vacation with Jesse's family. The small diving resort we were staying at was almost like our private playground. A beautiful oasis in the Caribbean, surrounded by white sand and crystal blue ocean, exactly like every postcard that was ever printed of a tropical beach.

Jesse and I, along with his brother and his wife, had made our way to the tiny beachside bar after dinner one night. Everleigh was only a toddler and too young to leave unsupervised. Her grandparents had already retired for the night and so we decided to bundle her up and put her to sleep on a lounge chair beside us. We were the only people at the bar, save for the bartender and his girlfriend. It was our own private party on the beach.

I had caught some kind of flu-like bug and felt a little under the weather, so at around 10 p.m. I asked Jesse to carry Everleigh to our room and I went to bed. I had expected him to show up a few hours later, most likely intoxicated and banging about the room with total disregard for anyone sleeping within a fifty-foot radius.

At around 3 a.m. I woke up feeling sick, and discovered I was alone with Everleigh in the room. Jesse was nowhere to be found. I panicked. He had no cell phone with him, because it didn't have service on the island so he'd left it on the dresser. I oscillated between fear and anger for hours. Daylight was creeping through the blinds when I heard him come in.

I was angry that he hadn't left a note and that he was drunk. But mostly I was angry because he had a habit of operating like a one-man show. He would follow his pleasure-seeking senses wherever they led him, then refused to acknowledge how it would make me feel. I would complain, be angry with him, he would attack, defend and justify himself. We would circle around each other, never able to resolve the rising conflicts.

I felt our roles slipping dangerously away from husband and wife and into that of parent and child. I resented it. I didn't want to be his mother. I didn't want a second child to be responsible for. I felt overburdened and so did he, but for different reasons.

Why did I, like so many other mothers I knew, have to be the ones who asked permission from their partners to briefly step away from their duties as a parent and wife, while for our husbands the thought wouldn't enter their minds? It seemed to me that every marriage I knew had suffered the same demise once their children had arrived. The mothers were worn out trying to hold it all together. Their mental, emotional and physical load had increased a hundred-fold and their husbands had barely acknowledged the shift. Husbands of every variety hadn't stopped playing team sports, hadn't stopped sleeping in to recover from a hangover, hadn't concerned themselves with carpooling, dentist appointments, packed lunches, after-school activities, and on and on. The mental load was immense and the resentment towards our partners seemed universal.

I had tossed about uneasily for hours before Jesse came stumbling into the room. I had plenty of time to dwell on my angry narrative; Mr Hyde had been out on a play date all night long and left his sick wife to handle their toddler. Again. Seemingly without any regard for anything but his own desires. His story was, he was on vacation in a beautiful place and he was going to milk every moment of his well-deserved break.

I quietly left the room at around 7 a.m. Jesse's family were not early risers and I was relieved to find myself alone at the breakfast buffet. I was in no mood for company. I had to quiet the anger and quell the sadness before I could manage any type of conversation. I was in a beautiful tropical place and eating by myself. I felt intensely lonely and wistfully observed other couples sitting together, picking food off each other's plates, bringing coffee back from the buffet. It was like Las Vegas all over again, but this time my husband's mistress wasn't the craps table, she was a beachside bar with plenty of shots.

I sat at the oceanside restaurant for over an hour, breathed in the sea air and began to soften a little as I relished the quiet moment with my book. Just before nine o'clock my mother-in-law arrived and settled opposite me with her milky coffee and meagre breakfast. She was a striking and formidable woman who had spent her career as an officer in the military. I loved her sense of humour and enjoyed her company, although we hadn't always seen eye-to-eye. We had misunderstood each other on several occasions and my freewheeling creative ways hadn't always conformed to her orderly and conservative manner. I felt I had been a character in too many confabulations, the product of harsh judgments and half-truths, it had made me cautious around her. Sometimes our conversations operated in this no-man's-land of general trust but with the uneasy knowledge that at any moment a sniper of accusation or judgment might send us running back to our trenches. We were fundamentally different, but I respected her and loved so many things about her.

At 9 a.m. Jesse was scheduled to take his first ocean dive after passing the PADI course. The stay was a gift from his mother and stepfather and most of the reason we were at this specific resort, known for its spectacular diving. His mother and stepfather were avid divers and looked forward to being able to share the experience. My mother-in-law was keen for him to enjoy his first dive and when she noticed the time approaching for him to leave, asked politely if I would fetch him from the room so he wouldn't miss the boat.

I had explained right before her request that I was alone because he was hungover and hadn't come home until daylight. I tried to control my anger with her son and not get into how tired I was of his repeated behaviour, but I was not about to leave my breakfast, walk across the beach to our room, climb the flight of stairs and collect our toddler so Jesse could make the dive. Nope. No, no, I was keen to let the natural consequences of his choices play out.

When I protested at enabling his shitty behaviour my mother-in-law lowered her voice, tilted her head to one side and said, "Honey, I know you're angry and if you won't do it for him, then do it for me."

I left the table having sullenly agreed only to meet Jesse walking halfway down the path toward us. He looked rough, but even when he looked rough he was annoyingly handsome. He brushed past me, barely acknowledging my presence, and headed straight for the coffee urn at the breakfast bar.

The rest of the vacation had been a struggle fraught with tension. I was craving the attention of the man I loved and wanted him to conform to a role I wasn't sure he would ever choose to play.

Many years after that incident, after the Me Too movement, I reflected on how many women I knew who had contributed to the dysfunctional patriarchy we were ruled by. Not in the way that they consciously discarded their own rights, but that it was often just easier to play along and "go with the flow".

It was how they were raised, and it fit neatly with the status quo. Generations of women were raised to be a "good girl" "good wife" "good mother" and if that meant their own needs and wants were trampled on, then their martyr- dom would be so much the richer. They were a product of social conditioning that praised selfless acts and honoured a woman who was willing to sacrifice her own desires in favour of putting her family's needs first. The generations who came after were freedom-seeking missiles who could see the chains of misogyny wrapped around their so-called freedoms. I was sick of the storyline that women had been sold, that our needs were secondary to the needs of our family, that to be "good" we must be selfless, that to have virtue we must deny our own dreams and be thankful for our lot in life. We must conform, comply and never complain.

Fuck. That.

Chapter 12

WHITE HIGH-TOPS

On the third week of Jesse's "leave of absence" from work, his phone rang. Every time I heard the ringer my heart would respond with an intense hammering. My throat would begin to close up and my stomach seemed to twist and contract. There had been nothing but bad news in the last few weeks and this call would be no different.

"So that's it?" he asked.

The conversation continued back and forth for a couple of minutes. I was getting ready to head to a doctor's appointment and trying to stay focused on the task at hand. "Keep moving forward," I told myself. "Left foot, right foot, left foot, right foot …" I created a rhythmic marching mantra to help steady the nerves and stay in the moment. If I was to stop for a moment and take it all in my system would overload. Jesse hung up. I didn't want to look, I didn't want to hear, not until I could armour up.

"They fired me," he said flatly.

He was in disbelief. His boss had fought hard for him to stay, had told him how sorry he was, but it came from the top. It was about the optics. They couldn't ignore the violence of his actions, The testimony and the video evidence presented by the mysterious neighbour was enough to seal his fate. They would pay him until mid-December.

There had been so many shocking incidents over the past few weeks, so much bad news to absorb, so much fear that had taken up residence, my body was at its breaking point. Our primary income was about to go up in smoke and I let the ensuing panic momentarily crush me.

But I had to move forward. I had to get to my doctor's office.

The small motions required to find my keys, grab my coat, put on my shoes, fill my water bottle, normally so simple, today they all required an enormous amount of focus.

I felt the panic try to take root and run riot with fearful thoughts. Every dark and desperate possibility tore through my mind. "Perhaps we'd be homeless." "What if he could never find work in his industry again." "Jesse will just want to end it all."

I felt my heart being held hostage by intense anxiety once more. But then I tied my shoes, white leather high-tops. I tied my shoes with deliberate focus and examined them with the curiosity of a toddler. I had shifted my focus with such determination that I was ensuring this latest wave of consequences would not take me out to sea. I had let the news float over me and hadn't let it settle.

Every motion from our loft to the parking garage was an exercise in mindfulness. My body had to pay attention to every sensation, otherwise I was going to be consumed by nausea and panic. I was hanging on by my fingernails and I couldn't let this latest information take me down. I had just enough access to my frontal lobe, where executive function lives, that I could engage my sensible inner therapist. She would be able to tame this savage beast of stress hormones into rational thinking. My inner dialogue went something like this: It's a job. He's always had a job. He'll find another job. So what if we accumulate some debt. We'll sell the loft. It's all fixable. This isn't the end of the world, Rachel. It's going to be okay.

I got into the car and appreciated its comfort. I pondered over the myriad of seating options and how I could personalize every detail. I touched the buttons on the stereo and marvelled at the hundreds of music choices I could access. I pulled out of the garage and for the half-hour journey stayed intently focused on every piece of external stimulus. I had finally outmanoeuvred shock. Perhaps it was the first stage of madness; perhaps it was denial; perhaps it was my best strategy. It was one I would need many more times over the coming months.

My doctor's office was in a small nondescript concrete building north of the city. It was a low-rise complex crammed with medical specialists of every variety and the attached parking lot was a one-way carousel that was like playing a slot machine. I would have to drive around and around the tight, narrow system and hope that someone was going to pull out right where I was cruising. This little game could take twenty minutes at times. But today, there was a space immediately in front of the building. I'd never been able to park right in front of the doors before. I decided to take this little insignificant coincidence as a personal message; it was the Universe telling me I would be accommodated, that it was going to be okay, that it wasn't always going to be a struggle. It was just a stupid parking spot, but I needed to keep shifting my mindset in a positive direction. I needed to think that all this chaos and drama was going to have happened for a reason. I needed to feel that forces I couldn't see could see me and that somehow my life was going to be enriched by this helter-skelter nightmare.

The small waiting room always smelled of disinfectant, which is precisely what you want your doctor's waiting room to smell like. Its vinyl floor tiles and neat rows of plastic chairs were positioned opposite the main desk. The desk where you check in for your appointment, the desk where you collect your orange-lidded container to pee in and the desk where you collected a face mask should you have a cough. I was at least grateful that when having you pee in a clear plastic container they had the good graces to accompany it with a brown paper bag. The space offered little anonymity, which had made me a bit uncomfortable during the days I had appeared on a lot of television shows.

The receptionist and nurse had recognized me and I was awkwardly uneasy about the fact that they would also know any and all of my medical conditions. But at least I had familiarity here; Dr Goldstein had been my doctor for almost twenty years. He was a yoga-practising father of three, with profound wisdom and a kindly yet efficient manner. He had seen me through a divorce, a re-marriage, a pregnancy and now this.

As I waited for him to arrive in one of the closet-sized exam rooms a female doctor walked in. She introduced herself as his resident and would I mind if she took down the details of why I was here today? As soon as she required me to speak, my words soldiered out like a ghostly echo of what I was feeling. Again I found myself dissociating. I couldn't attach "me" to what I was saying. I could only deliver a monotone report of the last couple of weeks. She typed away at the computer, furiously trying to keep pace, and I could tell that she was trying not to let a telltale inflection in her voice sound judgmental. It was a pretty sensational story and she was having a difficult time staying neutral.

By the time Dr Goldstein entered the room he had notes in hand. He had read the report she had just typed in his office. The three of us were small people in the space, but it was crowded. Dr Goldstein stood near the doorway as both available seats were taken.

He took a moment to take me in. I wasn't the usual cheerful, chatty patient who enjoyed cracking jokes about whatever ailed me. I was silent and my exhaustion was apparent. He was the kind of doctor who knew when his patients were struggling, when they were hanging on by a thread. He sighed and I wanted to sob. I wanted him to fix me, to fix everything.

"I've known you for twenty years,' he said softly, "and you know I'm never quick to write prescriptions, but you don't look like yourself. You don't look well and for once I think medicine might be able to help. If you would like the help?"

The man had such a deep respect for his patients and pills were always a last resort in certain lines of defence. I nodded and could say nothing more.

He handed me a prescription for antidepressants and I left in a newly induced haze, having just relived the last devastating few weeks.

I sat with the prescription in my wallet for the next few days. I had taken antidepressants once before, during the gambling phase. I had hated what they did to me, I had felt numb and decided that even feeling sad was better than feeling nothing at all. I knew that these pills might be different, but I couldn't bring myself to fill the prescription — not entirely because I was fearful of the outcome, but because I had begun to glide into some fleeting feeling that I really would be okay. I wondered if I could wrestle this into submission and enforce optimism like martial law. I wondered if I had it in me. Maybe a few rounds of Beyoncé cranked in my earphones could take the place of some medication. And maybe I was delusional. I was going to find out.

Chapter 13

HOODED COAT

Jesse and I encountered each other mostly in silence, keeping out of each other's way. My nerves seemed like they were on fire all the time and I ping-ponged around the apartment getting ready for my trip. Jesse shuffled zombie-like from room to room, sleeping and napping and reading. I had nothing to say. I had shifted my focus from hoping he would be something other than he was and instead fixated on my university application and getting my travel plans in order.

I had desperately wanted our marriage to work, but not under any circumstances. Not under the circumstances where he acted out in these toxic and dangerous ways without any acknowledgment of his impact, without remorse, without apology. I was tired of taking the mental and emotional beatings from Mr Hyde.

On one occasion I had even been on the receiving end of Mr Hyde's physical aggression. Jesse had characteristically denied and then downplayed the incident, leading me to question my own recollection of events. He was gaslighting me – a term coined after an old movie titled "Gaslight", where the abusive husband manipulates information so effectively that his wife is led to question her own sanity and grip on reality. It's a tactic I was all too familiar with as I recalled how my ex-husband had carefully taken a small element of truth and then woven a web of lies around it, obscuring it so thoroughly that I could hardly tell what the actual truth was. Suddenly playing a leading role in his theatre of the absurd was the most disorienting and unhinging feeling. Gaslighting is a powerful way to control a victim and it also insidiously keeps the focus off the perpetrator.

It had happened after a friend's Christmas party. Another bizarre series of events had unfurled that night. A few hours into the party, Jesse was swimming in righteous indignation over the presence of a guest he felt should not have been there.

Jesse had some cantankerous history with this guy. They had pursued me at the same time when I was newly single and Jesse had "won" the battle for my attention. They had had an uneasy dislike of each other ever since. It had come to light over the years that this guy didn't take no for an answer from women he had his sights set on. I had experienced him as something of a lecherous womaniser but friends of mine had seen a darker and more dangerous side of him. He would bully his way into their lives and their bedrooms and then became abusive when they rejected him. They had told me about some of the situations in confidence and I had been foolish enough to tell Jesse a watered-down version of events, knowing how much he already disliked this guy.

While I had not known at the time as I had been busy catching up with people at the party, Jesse saw fit to break those confidences that night. Due to his myopic drunken state and some sort of hero complex he had taken it upon himself to tell this guest that he had some balls showing up and wasn't welcome. Jesse knew what he was like, what he had done and what a snake he was. Jesse didn't consider the consequences of his words, the fallout of friendships, the broken trust and hurt feelings. He was going to make this guest aware that he was an asshole to women and that it would not be tolerated. The irony was not lost on me.

After several more rounds of "Christmas cheer" we left the party and hopped on the subway heading home. It was then I learned what had transpired between Jesse and the target of his rebuke. He began explaining it to me on the train and I was mortified. The consequences of his unwanted intervention began swirling and I knew that friendships would be broken. I certainly would be facing the completely justified outrage of friends who had confided in me delicate information that I had flippantly blabbed to my husband. I hadn't really expected him to even remember let alone take that information and use it as a weapon at a goddamn Christmas party!

As Jesse conveyed the details of his righteous admonishment my face registered how appalled I had felt. Jesse had then drawn his own conclusions about what I was thinking based on my expression. He concluded that I hated him (he wasn't entirely wrong in that moment). He also concluded, wrongly, that I didn't care about him, that I was looking at him with utter contempt. He also noted that I was obviously blind if I couldn't see that he had done everyone a favour by finally calling this guy out. I was overwhelmed by the consequences of what he had done.

We began to argue on the train but his escalating aggression over my disapproving response caused me to shut down. He was drunk. He leaned across his seat, head thrust inches away from my face and he spat, "I could punch you in the face right now." I felt as though I had left my body. In twelve years of our relationship he had never spoken to me like that, never looked at me with such animosity, and I had never felt threatened like I did in that moment. I couldn't wait to get some distance from him, from his temper, from the public eye and from the humiliation.

The train then came to an abrupt stop and we heard on the loudspeaker that it would no longer continue its expected journey. We would have to disembark and transfer to an awaiting shuttle bus above ground. I took my opportunity to separate myself from him and virtually ran from the train to the exit. I was wearing a coat with an oversized hood that I could pull around my face and avoid seeing anything other than a few feet in front of me. By the time I reached the bus Jesse was no longer behind me.

The seats filled up and I took a moment to collect myself and try to calm down. Right before the doors closed Jesse jumped on board, closely followed by a group of sober young men who seemed to be smiling at him. I had no idea what had happened and I had no intention of asking him. I had deliberately chosen a single seat to get away from him and his agitated confrontational mood. I was horrified at the thought of a public showdown with him.

It wasn't until days later that I learned what had happened as we left the train. A knife-wielding maniac had been thrashing around on the platform, being cautiously circled by a timid group of transit security officers. Jesse had witnessed the scene and in his inebriated frenzied state decided to tackle the perpetrator and snatch his knife away from him. It had taken him seconds to disarm the man. The transit cops were grateful for his swift intervention and in Jesse's mind he was a hero for the second time that night. He was now jacked up even more on a toxic combination of booze, adrenaline and testosterone.

I had missed the entire fiasco. Perhaps as a result of my panic in trying to distance myself and most certainly because I had worn my hood up with the intention of hiding away from the world, it had literally given me tunnel vision. Jesse had assumed I had seen it all: the man, the knife and the takedown. He assumed that my seemingly unconcerned and uncaring attitude towards him as I sat coolly in my single seat on the bus was because I really didn't love him or care if he lived or died. In my reality I had just been trying to avoid being humiliated by a belligerent drunk on public transport.

By the time we reached our stop I had already called an Uber to take us on the last leg of the journey and Jesse's outrage over my seeming nonchalance for his death-defying stunt had reached a fever pitch. He was not the type of man who would brag about being a hero, which compounded the stupidity of what was unfolding, him believing I had witnessed my heroic husband save the day but instead of gazing at him in awe I was looking at him with contempt. His brain addled by alcohol, he had logically concluded I was an uncaring bitch who was coldly unconcerned that he could've been stabbed and he was in disbelief that I was so self-absorbed about the fallout of my friendships. It was a situation that played perfectly into his ever-present narrative, "She doesn't love me like I love her." He was going to crush me before I crushed him.

I had slid over to the far side of the back seat of the cab in an effort to keep my distance from him and in so doing had ignited his fury. He consequently drew even closer and pinned me uncomfortably right up against the door. He was spitting insults at me as tears were streaming silently down my face and as I tried to apologise to the driver for the drama. I knew that engaging with Jesse in that moment and in that state would be like taking a match to a tinder box. But I was feeling a dichotomous combination of self-preserving resignation and a feral instinct to fight back.

Thankfully it was a short ride home and as soon as we pulled over I fled the car and ran for the safety of home. By this point Jesse had become consumed by rage. I had no way of knowing about the version of events he had just lived out and neither of us had the wherewithal to pause and ask questions about the other's perspective. All his self-righteous fury was about to reach a flash point.

He flew after me, punching walls and slamming doors so violently I thought they would come off their hinges. By the time I got into our apartment I was in a trembling mess of both terror and outrage. As we stood face to face in the kitchen, him still seething and spouting insults I finally snapped back. I grabbed his face with my one hand and yelled, "STOP! You need to fucking STOP!"

That move would almost cost us our relationship as for years afterwards Jesse would claim I had attacked him. Which from my perspective was an outrageous and ludicrous accusation, I had been trying to snap him out of it, make him pause and look me in the eyes. Besides which my hands are small and my strength miniscule compared to his towering athletic physique. Still, putting my hands on him was the last straw for him.

In a spilt-second I was off my feet, being carried across the room by his fist wrapped around the neckline of my coat. I remembered going limp and thought, this is how a small animal feels when its finally caught in the jaws of a predator. The pressure of his knuckles pushing into my sternum was knocking the wind out of me. With just one arm he had tossed me over the back of the couch so I was looking up at the ceiling with my feet higher than my head. My hair had flown past the coffee table and I was momentarily thankful my skull had missed it. If I had been a bit taller I would not have been so lucky. In just a few more seconds he had hauled me up again and grabbed me under the backs of my knees as if he was carrying a child. "You're going to bed!" he hollered. Then, he marched upstairs with me still in his arms and I was flung onto the bed.

The shock of it all was overwhelming. I contemplated calling the cops but quickly realised my phone was sitting on the kitchen countertop downstairs. Which may have turned out to be better in the long run anyway because I had time to pause and reflect on my options. There was no doubt I would have to call it quits now. I wasn't going to hang around and allow myself to be treated this way. This was beyond any rational person's tolerance. This was domestic abuse, plain and simple.

Yet, I stayed.

That night was the reason our marriage had been hanging by a thread for years. We had such entirely different perspectives on what transpired and our resentment of each other permeated every dispute. Whenever I attempted to raise the topic he would get defensive and would escalate into a volcanic state in minutes. The memory of it was too charged. Our marriage had become draped in the darkness of that evening and for years its resolution seemed an impossible onerous task.

The summer before the magic mushroom incident we had had a terrible fight that resulted in Jesse going to stay with his brother. During an attempted reconciliation phone call I had stated that I wasn't prepared to stay in a marriage where he believed that I deserved or provoked that violent outburst. I owned the fact that I shouldn't have grabbed his face and that I could have reacted different-ly. But his attack had left me with bruises on my arms, my legs and my chest, and a tiny scar on my hand where his watch had ripped out a chunk of skin. If I had somehow "deserved" that reaction in Jesse's estimation then I was done. If he adamantly refused to take ownership of his behaviour and deliver his so-called apologies with a "yeah-but" then I couldn't live with that.

I wanted my pain to be seen, I wanted to be heard, I wanted my sadness acknowledged, my reality validated. I wanted a heartfelt apology, no justifica-tion of his behaviour, no subtle air of victim-blaming. I wanted a sincere, meaningful "God I am SO sorry for what I did to you." It seemed highly unlikely that I was ever going to get one. The reason for which would not become apparent until many years on.

The words "I'm sorry" aren't a magic bullet of absolution. Especially when they don't acknowledge any wrongdoing, or pain caused and particularly when there is no intention of modifying future behaviour. A victim's pain is com-pounded when their perpetrator throws in some gaslighting. Subtle suggestions that you might be a little "excitable" or "prone to dramatization". Maybe you did something to deserve this, or maybe this is a pattern in relationships and you need to examine your role.

With enough repetition of these denouncing messages, the victim becomes psychologically disoriented and begins to question their own contribution to their antagonist's storyline. Gaslighting is excruciating, and the road to crazy-town is paved with liars and deniers.

Although I had lived through vicious gaslighting in my late twenties, the roots of my rage and the pain beneath could be traced all the way back to my childhood, where men were permitted to bully, to dictate, to be wildly insensi-tive, self-centred and domineering and never be called out. Where silence and resignation dominated every woman's response, a collective lassitude had settled over generations. Because single-handedly tackling systemic sexisim, racisim or any kind of embedded sense of superiority was a fight you just couldn't win. But such passive responses to blatant injustice isn't sustainable. It flies in the face of harmony, cooperation and progress. Eventually and inevitably a seething, sharp-toothed resentment would fester, hoping, praying, waiting for the patriarchy to crack. Waiting for the next generation to rise up, fists punching, middle fingers in the air, yelling, "Fuck you! I matter too!"

Jesse was exasperated by my inability to just let it go. My ex had said the same. Was I really that incapable of moving on? The answer was yes. I was holding in all the unspoken injustices, the years of witnessing, experiencing, feeling, all the shitty ways that men had been given permission to violate women. Like every woman I knew, I had lived through a spectrum of infractions, ranging from the wave of a hand to silence me in humiliating casual dismissal, to a childhood sexual assault. The weight I put on Jesse to see me, to deliver a meaningful apology was inextricably tangled in the mess of every violation. And the more I needed his acknowledgment the more he withdrew. I was too needy, too demanding, the validation too necessary for him not to feel exasperated by me. My compounded sadness and sense of injustice too big for either of us to navigate.

I wanted Dr Jekyl to confront Mr Hyde, talk sense to him and show him the error of his ways. I wanted the kind and thoughtful Jesse to be present even under the influence of whatever substance he felt he needed to flirt with. I wanted the man I knew was buried beneath his own pain. But like so many other men, he knew no other way of handling powerful negative emotion except with anger. They weren't raised by a society that allowed their expression of pain in anything other than machismo-fuelled outbursts. Substance abuse was a cheap and convenient therapy; they could forget themselves for a while, allow their alter egos to take control and fuck the consequences.

Jesse's own father was a real-life G.I. Joe, part of an elite group of specially trained military men called SAR-Tech's, search and rescue technicians who would risk their own lives to save others. A group of well-trained and fearless adrenaline junkies who would jump out of airplanes into insanely dangerous circumstances. Not exactly the type of men to sit around a campfire after a rescue and sing "Kumbaya" as they processed their emotions. They had no time for the notion "you gotta feel it to heal it" — that was a luxury reserved for those who didn't have to function under an emergency call. Besides, it was decades before we had any awareness of how traumatising this kind of work could be for first responders. Their coping mechanism of choice was alcohol, and it was the perfect companion for the "suck it up buttercup" mentality.

Jesse was a product of his father's influence and of the prevailing attitude towards men of his and previous generations, the "big boys don't cry" generations. Men who had suffocated their pain until it was entirely numbed by way of intoxication. Men who internalized the weight of every unresolved trauma and the accumulation of slights and infractions, big events or trifling annoyances. The only option their social conditioning would permit was to "man up".

As a consequence of this dysfunctional thinking, families became collateral damage as the men tried to seek relief from their own demons. It was no wonder to me that this crisis of thought accompanied another dysfunctional facet of a heavily weighted patriarchal society, that men would seek relief from the internalized pain using whatever method they could. They had no helpful tools, no meaningful strategies, no healthy coping mechanism and no permission to express themselves any other way other than toxically.

Jesse's pattern of drinking and abusive behaviour didn't come marching into our lives like a thrashing, maniacal outlaw. It waltzed in slowly, like a charming, well-dressed salesman. Besides, Mr Hyde was not a dominant character in our daily lives. I knew when he was likely to appear, like the ringmaster in a travelling circus, the blazing red tailcoat and towering top hat creating the showman for only a few hours. He confused me. I loved Jesse and all his thoughtful, giving ways. Separating Jesse from his unacceptable behaviour and balancing my love for him with my own self-preservation would not be shoved into a black and white box of reductive reasoning. It was complicated, like every marriage. It's easy to speculate on the rights and wrongs of a relationship from the disentangled sidelines, but like the root system of an ancient tree, the growth above ground was only possible and visible because of what had developed below the surface.

I had never known Jesse to be as still and reflective as he was during the stagnant days after being fired, when he escaped into the pages of Daemon's book. His tall and capable body lay sunken into the couch for hours. The book held hovering above his face like a mesmerizing hummingbird hoping his new insights would be like a hit of sweet life-sustaining nectar. A silent observer, I witnessed him slowly unravelling. His sadness and the weight of his pain was going to crack him open and this breakage would be necessary for him and for everyone who loved him. But like all evolution, it was a slow and messy process. The change required to keep our family together would be significant. He would have to learn to stay in the discomfort of painful conversations, learn the language of vulnerability and adopt new ways to cope. We'd moved beyond the incubation period and were in the phase of rebirth, the wailing, sticky, bloody and forceful push into a new paradigm.

Chapter 14

COATS AND BACKPACKS

A few weeks before Christmas, the airport was predictably teeming with people. I always found airports to be fascinating, every traveller a rich and exquisitely different piece of the patchwork of humanity. I wanted to know every story that trailed through the gleaming white hallways of Pearson International: Why were they traveling? Who were they visiting? Who were they leaving behind?

I was glad to be travelling alone. Usually I had Everleigh in tow and although she was already an excellent and seasoned traveller who had taken her first flight at just two months old, I was enjoying the freedom to think of no one but myself. As with virtually every mother of a young child, the option to visit a bathroom unaccompanied, or sip a coffee before it turned cold, or simply sit alone with your thoughts was as luxurious to me as checking in at any five-star resort.

I had ten days in England and I was going to make every moment an essential piece of the track I would lay down for my new life. I would arrive in Manchester on Friday, take the two-hour trip to the small village where my parents lived in the Yorkshire countryside, and be ready for a university tour on Monday. I had set it up a week or so before. My application was in and I was intending to ferret out anyone I could find from the psychology department and help them remember my name. I wasn't going back to school for fun, I was going because my future depended on it. I was going to walk the delicate line between pushy and persuasive. I would be my usual chatty, good-humoured self and lock away the drama of the last few weeks.

My mum and I arrived in Sheffield in plenty of time for the campus tour. I was glad to have her company for this epic life transition. I felt my white-knuckle grip around life beginning to ease in the company of my parents. They would give anything they had for us to be safe and happy. Their presence was the elixir for all the disorder and disquietude. The sharp edges of my life were smoothed in the company of people who truly supported me, people who would willingly and without question travel for days to be by my side in times of need. A realization would make me deeply sad, that when I returned back to Canada I would be without them, without the supportive net of connectivity so vital in this isolating and volatile situation.

We stepped off the tram into the historic streets of the northern town. The rich history of Sheffield was immediately evident. A once-thriving industrial hub famous for Sheffield steel and where stainless steel was invented, the city has been inhabited since circa 9000 BCE.

Being back in England after so many years of living abroad was like looking through a technicolour lens. My appreciation for its history and its architecture had never been so intense, recognizing the layers of time made manifest in every variety of building.

The crisp December morning made for a chilly walk to the campus. The university sprawled across the city landscape, its buildings evident by the flocks of students gathered around them. We located an information desk and gathered a map and instructions on where to meet for the tour. With some time to spare, we decided to sit at a bustling cafe for a mid-morning snack and a hot drink.

The cafe was crammed with people, students and professors alike, somehow comfortably squashed around the small tables, patrons amiably manoeuvring between chairs overflowing with winter coats and backpacks. As we sat, I enjoyed what felt like an ordinary moment, a normal occurrence of sipping coffee and soaking up the scene. There was nothing lurking in the shadows, no sinister announcement that could leap out from around the corner and terrorize me for days. The panic at my epicentre had subsided, if only briefly.

The campus tour gathered in the lobby of a modern and energetic building. I wanted to stand silent in the entrance and drink in the coruscating sunlight as it filtered through the gleaming windows. We toured the campus with fresh-faced students, eager to share their vibrant oasis and we marvelled at every little thing. Sheffield University had twirled onto the pages of the otherwise dark and unsettling screenplay that was my current life. Hope was alive here and possibility was seated at every corner, confidently swinging her crossed legs into the future. I felt fortified by hope and I knew I belonged here. Little did I know that in the months to follow I would discover my body had other plans in store for me, and my storyline would move in a completely unexpected direction.

At the end of the campus tour a friendly and efficient member of the recruitment team informed me that there was an interview day scheduled for 9 a.m. the next morning and would I be interested in participating. If it would improve my chances of being accepted then I was absolutely interested. She took my email address and said she would send me details of what would be covered as soon as she could.

That night I lay in bed and just before going to sleep checked my email one final time to see if anything had come through about the interview day. There it was. In my inbox a detailed outline of what we would be covering. I sat up like a meerkat standing to attention. The list of subjects included a forty-five-minute exam on algebra, statistics, integers and other math-related topics I had long forgotten. There was also an English exam and four separate interviews with various departments of the university.

Sleep would have to wait. I grabbed a pen and paper and began to search YouTube for math tutorials.

I got a few hours' sleep and was still studying on the train the next morning. I felt strangely relaxed, a little anxious about the math portion of the schedule but I had done what I could to better my chances. The professor giving the orientation had noted that she was aware that most people had had two weeks to prepare but some had been given less than twenty-four hours notification and might also be suffering from jet lag. I was so thankful that I had been seen in this way, that she at least recognized the struggle.

I fumbled my way through the math exam and actually enjoyed the English portion. I felt confident about the face-to-face interviews and when it was over I was buoyed up with a sense of achievement. It had been a long time since I had felt a sense of pride and accomplishment. I also felt like I was taking back some control over the direction of my life.

I arrived back in Canada feeling optimistic about my trip, but also wondering if the exams and interviews would be enough to tip the scales of my future. It would be a long few weeks of waiting until I received an early-morning email just a few days before Christmas. I had been accepted. We were visiting Jesse's family and I wasn't sure how the news would be received. I decided to take an early morning walk and ponder the ramifications. Walking had become a vital component to my sanity. Pacing away my anxiety was giving me access to at least a little relief. This was going to be a huge step.

Jesse was proud of me, even happy for me. Was he happy we were going to have to live apart for four years? Was he happy we would be taking a break? Or just happy that I'd been accepted? I decided not to drill down into his response. It ultimately would make no difference. Besides, I had over nine months to prepare for the September start and plenty could unfold between now and then. As it turned out, while I was thinking about our lack of finances and the possibility of Jesse's jail time, I had no idea what was truly about to unfold.

The news wasn't easy to deliver to Jesse's family. To my disappointment it was met with a stony reception by all but one. I was both saddened and angered by their collective response. This was a big accomplishment; the university was ranked in the top one hundred in the world and the hoops I had to jump through to make this happen were extraordinary under the circumstances. Circumstances their own family member had created. I felt undeserving of their apparent disapproval. I figured most women would have packed their bags and closed the door for good. At least I was trying to better myself, to better our future, to work hard and do what I needed to do. At least I wasn't giving up and letting myself collapse.

It wasn't until some time had passed that I understood that they may also be feeling grief — for our marriage, for the tragedy that created this and for the grandchild and niece that would be four thousand miles away. Their feelings about it would never really come to light, but I suspected that Jesse's mum had understood more than she was willing to say.

As my future marched forward, Jesse's played alongside in an obscure pantomime of unpredictability. His lawyer had told him to visit a psychiatrist and an addictions counsellor. Daniel needed to know who his client was, and the court would be looking closely at the findings. The sessions with his doctor came with a hefty price tag and the financial stress of the situation harkened back to the mad days of 2001 living with a chronic gambler. I wanted Jesse's sessions with his team of medical professionals to yield some kind of epiphany for him. I had delusional expectations that he would come home "fixed". He didn't. He continued to read, to sleep, to be mostly silent.

He occasionally shared a passage from the book, however, and it was evident that something was happening. Some sort of softening was occurring within him; some level of humility was starting to seep into his being. I pondered the serendipity of having that random conversation with my neighbour that led to this book being in our apartment. Was it meant to be here? Was all of this supposed to happen? Was it all going to reveal a greater purpose? Or was it all just shit-bad luck?

It wasn't too long after Christmas that Jesse started a new job, one that allowed him to work from home and set his own pace. He also began volunteering as part of his effort to make amends, and periodically received phone calls from Daniel to update him on his case. His female victim was an educated and politically active woman, a mother of young children, and she wasn't interested in anything other than seeing him go to jail. Although I had my own terror about seeing Jesse behind bars and how devastating it would be for Everleigh, I couldn't blame her. I didn't blame her; she had done absolutely nothing but be in the wrong place at the wrong time. Yet I felt so helpless once again, that my life might be turned upside down, this time by a complete stranger who had every right to send my husband to jail.

Chapter 15

STRAITJACKET

Jesse thumbed the pages of Daemon's book over and over, reading and re-reading the most meaningful passages to me and back to himself. It had resonated deeply and taken root in his psyche. It was remarkable to me that words on a page had the power to cast such a spell on the reader. The power even to change a mind or to soften a perspective, to bring insight where there was blindness and to mellow a hardened heart. He was cultivating new thoughts, the words on the page generating new possibilities. There was hope here at last.

Jesse gradually stopped defending and justifying his misdeeds. His guilt had tied him up so tightly that he would not allow himself to fully see the pain he had caused. He couldn't forgive himself for the things he had done and therefore shut himself off, rendering himself incapable of feeling beyond his own failures. His guilt had made a travelling companion of shame and when shame was in the room the conversation would go nowhere. Jesse would throw up his hands and simply leave, often in a rage.

He found it impossible to stay in a difficult dialogue because the pain became unbearable. My tenacity in the pursuit of a genuine apology and my aching for a bona fide acknowledgment of the ways he had damaged us all — me, his family and even complete strangers was, for him, like a squeeze of lemon in an open wound. It was drilling down into his guilt and shame until he couldn't bear it. And then because I was left still wounded and raw, so the cycle seemed as if it would never end.

Jesse had a tattoo on his shoulder blade that he'd had done the minute he turned eighteen. It was a bull's head, in part because he was a Taurus, which is symbolised by the bull, and partly because he would refer to his alter ego as "The Bull". The reference had annoyed me because I had seen it as a way of deflecting personal responsibility, blaming something outside of himself. But what I had failed to understand was The Bull was a necessary manifestation born of a soft-hearted little boy who wanted everyone to "play nice and get along" but who had been damaged by cruelty and had his kindness betrayed. It was his protective shield, an essential part of his armour.

Poetically the bull tattoo had begun to fade over the years, taking on a softer, more velvety appearance. The result of the constant regeneration of new skin and the abrasive effects of a life at the halfway point.

Jesse would reveal to me many years past the subway incident that The Bull was in charge that night because he had witnessed the woman he loved so deeply and completely being more concerned about the state of her friendships than for his safety. Instead of allowing his pain to be expressed in a humiliating public show of tears, he had become enraged and used his fists to release his agony.

When we were finally able to hear each other's perspective of what had happened that night, we both softened towards each other. I understood more about the depth of his pain and his ensuing wrath. He understood that my attention was focused on my friendships rather than on him because I simply hadn't witnessed him tackling the guy with the knife. It was a such a poignant revelation that had sprung from an inane and elemental misunderstanding.

Daemon was able to reach him through the pages of his book by offering compassion, insight, reason and most importantly, empathy. Jesse was a softie behind his Marlboro Man exterior; he was a tender and sensitive boy. A man

who, it seemed to me, was another victim of social conditioning and perni-
cious stereotypes. The way he was wired and the way the world had told him
he should be wired were often in excruciating opposition. Consequently, the
tendrils of shame had woven themselves into every fibre of his being and
empathy would be the only remedy that could set him free.

Every gentle, tender, sensitive man I'd ever known was a tortured soul
imprisoned by ridiculous characterizations of how we wanted manhood served
up. Bombarded by images of muscular, athletic vigilante superheroes, or aloof
and lonesome cowboys, or, swashbuckling, murderous pirates, we had consumed an endless carousel of dysfunctional personalities, a dramatis personae
of a world gone mad.

My heart ached for all the sweet souls who had been buried under the rubble
of destructive machismo. I had often thought that the most sensitive men were
frequently the most badly behaved, caught in a ridiculous straitjacket of
conformity that only permitted "manly" expressions of feelings. The sensitive
ones could see that the world was on fire and responded appropriately. But the
world would punish them for their vulnerability; they would need to toughen
up to steer their lives appropriately. They would never be able to lead, to
conquer, to rule, to "be a man" if they were kind, thoughtful, gentle, sensitive,
compassionate or, God forbid, had the notion that they should acknowledge
their feelings.

What if these were the men who would never have come unhinged if they
had been given permission to express their feelings? What if they had been
allowed to emote beyond the confines of the artificial construct of imprisoning
acceptable rules? What if they had never been told to "man up", "suck it up",
"buck up", "get up"? What if they had been given the language to name their
feelings instead of deny them? What if their alcoholism, drug abuse, gambling
addiction, dysfunction of every variety, could have been avoided if society had
encouraged their sensitive insights and not labelled them a sissy?

Despite the heart-warming signs of change, I couldn't yet invest in Jesse's transformation. I could only stay fixated on my own future and let him fully metamorphosize at his own pace. He had shown me some signs of reform, but this was after I'd already experienced fourteen years of lukewarm apologies that never led to lasting change.

I wanted to hope. I wanted to dream. I wanted that Hollywood ending. But I was too afraid and still too angry. Yet my anger had helped propel me out of helplessness. It had given me the energy I needed to apply to university, to sit the exams, to get up and fight for my future and for Everleigh's. I was glad to have already traversed the landmines of ever-present uncertainty, financial ruin, debilitating fear, sleepless nights, crippling nausea, heart palpitations and all the other side-effects of a personal crisis. Yet, for the very same reasons I was glad to have built up resilience, I had also built a wall of protection. It was too early to predict if that wall could be dismantled.

The next few months would see our bank accounts drain as the legal fees mounted into a back-breaking five-figure debt. Every bill towards his defence made me angry, but I was resolute that this would not dictate the tone of my future. I was getting better at allowing the panic to wash over me. I was learning to witness my fearful emotions from a distance and not become embroiled in them. I was practicing stepping outside of myself, imagining that I was simply a puppet on a stage and the real me was in the audience, observing, but not heavily invested in its characters or its outcome. I made the conscious decision to "zoom out" like this several times a day.

Chapter 16

ARMOUR

I had been trying to keep Everleigh's life as stable and normal as possible, though at times I felt like the wizard in The Wizard of Oz, wondering if she would discover me hiding behind the curtain and suffer the pain of disillusionment. She had been struggling in school since before the incident and I was dedicating a lot of my energy to getting her the help that she needed. The school system was over-burdened and under-resourced, like in every country that didn't prioritize and value education and teachers. It would be another exhausting fight for me to take on, but after many months of championing her cause she was getting the allotted forty-five minutes of additional weekly help. A meagre reward for the dozens of emails and in-school meetings that took place, but it was the most the school could offer, and it was at least setting her on the right path.

Everleigh was happier now that the difficulties with her reading and writing were known and she was being properly accommodated. I was determined to be a good and effective advocate for her. I myself had come careening off the rails at the age of seventeen, overwhelmed by struggle until I became suicidal. What I had needed most was someone to advocate for me, someone to help me navigate the feeling of being overwhelmed I had felt for years. My history has always hovered over my parenting style, a quiet tiny droplet of terror that floated around my inner world, whispering, "She might come undone, just like you. Better make sure you don't lose her."

The one loss I knew I would never be able to overcome would be the loss of my child. I knew a number of families who had lost a child either to suicide, drugs or car accidents and I had felt a subsequent hollowness in the parents I could barely consider. Whether I lost her physically or emotionally, the thought was equally painful. It was an exclusive club I never wanted a membership to.

Jesse's strategy throughout Everleigh's difficulties was mostly to tell her to work harder. He had infuriated me for his lack of insight and his nonchalance towards her needing special assistance. His approach was essentially the equivalent of telling her to man-up: work harder, don't be a whiner, don't be lazy, get off your ass and fix it. He was simply regurgitating the mindless doctrine we have all been a victim of at one point or another.

I, on the other hand, would become the school board's equivalent of Sigourney Weaver in the movie Alien, clad in a ferocious and deadly contraption of armour and menacingly calling on the killing machine. I would fight for her because I would not let her come derailed down the line if there were anything I could do to prevent it. I wouldn't allow the seeds of self-destruction to take root just because her struggles hadn't been seen in time. I would not let her confidence slip through the cracks like mine had.

Jesse didn't take on a fight like I did. He looked for immediate solutions and if they weren't available, he would abandon the cause in favour of a cigarette. And often, his release of the situation would yield a solution. He was annoyingly sanguine when I was spinning out, trying to force answers into being. I tackled a problem with a ferocity and tenacity that made me a force to be reckoned with, a characteristic that had both helped me succeed in life and that could make me intense and difficult to be around. A little of his influence would be a powerful antidote to the pressure I put on myself and others to bend an outcome to my will.

However, Everleigh was my baby and there would be no sitting back and allowing the problem to resolve itself. My history had told me that wasn't possible, and my quiet inner terror would always scare me into action. I was a cliché in motion, a mother on the warpath, willing to do whatever was necessary for her baby to get the help she needed. Why did we have to advocate so hard for our children's education, in a country as prosperous as Canada? My battle for Everleigh would be just another fight that would ready me for the next reckoning, another life-changing moment that lay quietly metastasizing.

Chapter 17

SMART CASUAL

Jesse and I plodded through our days as the weather began to turn and the intensity of the Canadian summer came crashing into the atmosphere. People would tell me they loved the four seasons of the Canadian climate, but in my estimation, there were two seasons, viciously cold and searingly hot. If you weren't paying attention, Spring and Autumn would flash by like a figment of imagination.

I tried not to complain about my life, despite the circumstances; complaining simply never made me feel better. But I complained about the weather, freely and to anyone. I hated the extremes of temperatures, sometimes fluctuating a full twenty degrees in one single day. It wasn't fashion- or hair-friendly and I was always mildly uncomfortable and irritated at having to switch from winter boots immediately into sandals, there would be no time for cute lace-ups or booties in this climate.

Jesse had completed his psyche evaluations with flying colours. His counsellors had deemed him a well-adjusted individual and not a threat to society. Daniel had been keeping tabs on his progress and we had continued to fill the coffers of Daniel's expensive downtown office, hoping that it would be enough to keep Jesse out of jail. Despite the looming shadow of life-changing uncertainty, we were moving forward. We were finding ways to reconnect. We spent our days in quiet conversation. Neither of us had the energy for the hostile volleys we had once engaged in. Jesse had reckoned with his albatross of shame, and anger had loosened its grip around my throat. Either resignation or surrender had settled over us, and we were comfortably worn out.

The periodic calls from Daniel always caused my heart to pound, harbingers of doom my body couldn't ignore. I was like a Pavlovian dog: the phone would ring and uncontrollable fear would ricochet through me. My only defence was to acknowledge the response and know that it would pass. Whatever the news was, I would move past it. This was the stuff that resilience was made of, a tight-knit chain mail of moments of terror¬ — seen, felt and overcome.

During one of these calls Daniel told Jesse that his victim was willing to enter into mediation. She had been persuaded by the judge to consider a dialogue. She was understandably resistant but had ultimately agreed. The judge had wanted to avoid sending Jesse to jail, as it would cause generational pain and suffering. The news had offered a glimmer of hope. I was grateful to the judge, grateful to Jesse's victim and hopeful that somehow healing would find her way to them and wrap them up in an understanding embrace.

Jesse was contacted by the mediators, who asked him to meet with them at a local coffee shop. The casualness of the arrangement seemed peculiar to me, but I supposed the atmosphere of a café would help them to connect; it would be less formal and certainly less intimidating than the admonitory atmosphere of an imposing Bay Street office tower. It would be the three of them — two mediators, a man and a woman, and Jesse. They would hear his side of the story, they would need to get to know him, and then would make their recommendations to the court. He was to meet them at 7 p.m.

I helped him choose his outfit, as I always did, carefully evaluating each piece of clothing with the accuracy of the message he was trying to convey. Jeans, a collared shirt and a V-neck sweater in neutral tones, casual but respectfully smart and appropriate for the coffee shop that I had previously googled for reference.

It wasn't the five-dollar-a-shot type of coffee shop that dominated Toronto street corners; this one was old school, one of the originals that hadn't been gentrified with a hand carved live-edge bar and uniformed baristas. This was a coffee shop with years of dubious characters wandering in and out, wearing thin the 1980's black and white tiled floors and sitting wearily on the black and red vinyl chairs.

As Jesse left for the meeting I reached for my earphones and cruised my playlist in search of a panacea. I had often used music as my drug of choice to find a sympathetic echo chamber for my unmanageable feelings. I had read that if you could find a piece of music whose harmony was able to match your emotional state just one level more upbeat than you felt, that it would offer relief. I had found that notion to be true and often used music to propel me into a happier state of being. When I looked back at the dark and brooding days of my teenage depression I had been obsessed with The Cure and Pink Floyd's The Wall. They had resonated with me and spoken to me with their lyrics, breaking the chains of the confining English proclivity to be silent about our emotions. They were symbols of freedom of expression and were defiant and rebellious, thrusting a middle finger in the face of British stoicism.

Perhaps it was then that music had become an extension of my voice, offering an acceptable expression of all the knotted-up intensity of big feelings whose expression, had they come from my own mouth, would have been met with disapproval and raised eyebrows. Music had long been the voice of my soul and the storyteller of my inner world. Dance-able Indie pop was my elixir of choice as Jesse made the short trip to the coffee shop.

At around 9 p.m. he called me to say that the meeting was going very well and that the mediators were hopeful that they would be able to bring him face-to-face with his victim at some point down the line.

Chapter 18

PILL BOX HAT

Jesse and I decided to send Everleigh to be with my parents for six weeks in the summer. I had collected enough air mile points to trade for her ticket. We wanted her to have the experiences only Europe could offer and to have the precious memories that I had had of spending time alone with my grandparents. She was excited by the idea, although apprehensive about flying alone for the first time. I had assured her that the crew would take care of her every need. But I was being the Wizard of Oz once again, selling her the best possible outcome, though unable to guarantee it would be delivered. My own experience of flying alone at the same age as Everleigh was something of an epic failure.

Circa 1980 we lived in New Delhi, India and I was going to spend the summer holidays with my grandparents back home in the UK. The flight had been a red-eye direct from Delhi to Heathrow, with a quick onboarding in Karachi. I was flying Thai Airways, whose flight crew of cheery, smiling, nodding attendants didn't understand much English and I certainly didn't speak any Thai. But what would it matter? I would be getting on a plane and getting off a plane, a simple exercise that required little communication. My parents had delivered me into the hands of a Thai Airways flight attendant around midnight and then went home, believing I would wind up in my grandmother's arms nine hours later.

New Delhi was a steaming hot chaotic city, an enmeshment of people, dogs, cows, cats, chickens — virtually any two- or four-legged creature could be seen and smelled at every hour of the day. The rickshaws, buses and bicycles were all obscenely and dangerously overloaded with bodies, each of them hollering, honking and screeching to their destinations. The airport was simply a microcosm of the city chaos — unbearably hot, disorganized hustle and bustle.

The obliging flight attendant sat me beside an older gentleman who turned out to be English too and, as we would discover after a brief introduction, we shared the same last name. An extraordinary coincidence on a plane full of people from every corner of the globe.

It was the middle of the night when I awoke to the sound of a bell being rung in my ear. The flight attendant had been holding a small brass handbell stamped with the word "Thai" in an elaborate cursive font and enthusiastically shaking it until I woke up. She gestured to me that I must get off the plane with everyone else and I had thought, "Wow, that was fast! I fell asleep and now we're in London!" But as I followed the trail of weary passengers to the exit door I discovered we were still in the oven-like heat of the New Delhi summer and hadn't moved from the tarmac.

At that age I slept deeply and didn't wake up quickly. In a catatonic-like state of awareness, I tried to gather my wits. Attached to an exit door was a precarious looking metal staircase and the scene below was mayhem. There were bags and suitcases scattered all over the tarmac, as if someone had tossed them like confetti from the back of the plane. I saw people dragging their luggage to an awaiting vehicle and loading their cases onto the flatbed trailer. I wandered zombie-like in the darkness looking for my case. When I found it I couldn't lift it, so I shuffled and pushed and heaved it inch by inch towards the trailer. A young British couple saw me struggling and came to my aid. The woman spoke to me with such kind concern I wanted to cry. I was so tired and confused about what was going on. She and her husband walked me back up the metal staircase where she spoke with the flight attendant who nodded and smiled and led me back to my seat beside the man they must have assumed was my grandfather.

We had been delayed for about eight hours. Meanwhile my grandmother had been pacing the airport since the small hours of the morning and her nerves were frayed. She had tried to get information about my flight, and no one had given her anything resembling a satisfactory answer. In fact, they had alarmed her into a DEFCON 1 state by telling her I wasn't even on the plane; they had no record of me. In true form, my grandmother had decided not to call my parents in the middle of the night thereby setting off their own nuclear panic. She relentlessly tried to figure out what had happened to me when there was an announcement over the airport loudspeakers.

"Would Mrs Davies please come to the British Airways information desk immediately."

Our flight finally landed in the beehive of Heathrow in the middle of the day. The kindly old gentleman seated beside me bid his farewell and tottered off down the aisle, leaving me to gather my things and be on my way. As I left the plane I saw a group of kids also disembarking. They were all huddled together around a flight attendant and carrying Thai Airlines activity kits. I remember feeling so excluded and bewildered, like my addled brain must not be understanding something. I was exhausted and not sure where to go next, so I decided to follow the herd of passengers from my flight, which was a good strategy until they dispersed into innumerable directions. I was left standing in the middle of Heathrow, clutching my passport with a sudden frisson of despair rippling through me.

I have always wanted to believe that there is some kind of divine order in our world. Some form of celestial stewards looking out for us, whispering in our ears, prompting us to move in one direction or another with the gentle wand of intuition. The next moment played out as if the hand of God himself had decided to step in and redirect the scene. Like he was watching it unfold, one-eyebrow cocked in disbelief and thinking, "Whoa, wait a minute, this needs a little intervention." Cue the whistle to summon this kid's angels.

I spun around and around, like a clichéd movie scene where the character begins to lose control, then seemingly as if she had sprung up between the cracks of the tiled floor was an impeccably uniformed British Airways flight attendant. Her blond hair was neatly pinned into a low bun that sat below her navy-blue pillbox hat. She had a broad and cheerful smile and asked me sweetly, where I was going, where were my parents and where was I travelling from? I had answered all questions politely and with a huge sense of relief that someone had come to my aid. She listened to me carefully and then took my hand. The recollection of her care and kindness still overwhelms me decades on.

She asked if I had a passport and took it from me, assuring me she would keep it safe. Still holding me by the hand, she radioed for a golf cart to pick us up. Succoured and comforted by my angel in a navy-blue uniform and Union Jack neck scarf, I boarded the golf cart with her. I felt the relief and the thrill of bouncing through the airport with my new heroes, the attendant and the driver who whipped us between pedestrians with immense speed and agency.

First stop, the luggage carousel to collect my suitcase, and then to a desk with a Thai Airways sign hanging over it. She gave me a quick assurance that she would be right back and then strode ferociously towards the two unsuspecting attendants on the other side of the counter. My view from the golf cart was of the smiling faces of the Thai employees gradually turning wide-eyed and panicky as my Navy-Blue Angel, gesticulating wildly, let them have it. She was my first real-life Joan of Arc.

Our golf carting adventure ended at the British Airways information desk, where my angel made the announcement seeking my grandmother. I was rescued and my grandmother looked at the point of collapse when she finally laid eyes on me. Now she would call my parents.

Weeks after that we discovered the plane had been delayed because of a suspected bomb on board and in looking for it, the luggage had been unceremoniously turfed out of the cargo hold. Such was the way in New Delhi circa 1980. I sure as hell was glad for tighter security in 2019, but my stomach still flipped when I thought of that memory and my baby boarding the plane by herself.

Everleigh had been making lists for days and had packed her backpack in characteristic fanatical order. The day of her flight she wore her near-fluorescent hoodie (you must be easy to spot in a swarm of people), bright blue leggings (the next best things to pj's for a red-eye flight) and sneakers with Velcro (easy to adjust to any swelling and quick to take on and off).

When July 23rd rolled around our little family of three boarded the train for the airport and Jesse and I shared the experience of slight apprehension at relinquishing our little adventurer. We handed her over to the fresh-faced millennial flight attendant and I asked her at least three times if she would be staying with her until they boarded. Everleigh had always made friends quickly and within minutes was happily waving us goodbye and chatting with her chaperone by her side. I said a silent prayer for my now deified Navy Blue Angel to watch over her.

Chapter 19

SOFT CARDIGANS

Once Everleigh had safely arrived in England, Jesse and I carried on with life without incident. We were finally able to have frank and honest conversations without the vitriol and intensity they had once possessed. His willingness to face the consequences of his actions and the ruminative state he had entered into allowed us to have a deeper, more honest connection.

As eight years his senior and a chronically responsible person I had arrived at certain conclusions about myself and life much sooner than he had. Jesse had a carpe diem approach, and the value of self-reflection had evaded him. Thinking too deeply for him was a waste of energy when life was calling him to participate. I was the antithesis of his spontaneous, insouciant soul.

Post-eight years of therapy, a bookcase of self-help books and countless pages of chicken-scratched stream-of-consciousness writings, I had acquired some insights about myself and, as therapists like to call it, my family-of-origin story. I had always understood that the past is the essential knitting together of what forms us in the present and understanding more about my own history had given me access to deep realms of self-compassion. When Jesse refused to look back, refused to examine his past, he had denied himself and our marriage crucial insights and solicitude.

I was a very sensitive child, always deeply contemplative and would often be described as "serious". I could walk into a room and feel all the feelings, an immense burden and a crushing conundrum for a kid being raised in a culture that had actively repressed the expression of emotions.

Over time, I had been bound by the stories I had allowed others to tell about me. Not having developed the wisdom or confidence to determine where their story ended and mine began. I had allowed people and society to tell me that being so sensitive was an acute disadvantage in a world that valued toughness, ambition, self-reliance. The attributes necessary to succeed in life required a level of thick-skinned insensitivity. I had allowed my rich and vibrant inner world of intense emotion to become something to be ashamed of. I had been told that competition was favoured over cooperation in business and not to give away too much. I had been too this, or not enough that, and I had bought into their storytelling until I had come undone.

Like so many creative and sensitive people I knew, I had lived up to the trope of tortured, insecure artists. Very often we had been born into families who had suffered generational trauma, silently and unconsciously absorbing the wounds of our parents. Wounds that had caused the entire family to retreat from the world and snarl with mistrust at strangers like an abused dog. The unspoken truths, the dysfunctional, numbed-out, shut-down feelings the tribe had silenced because their survival depended on it, these were passed down to the children without intention or awareness. The sensitive child's presence in such a family was like an atomic bomb disrupting the surface tension of an icy smooth lake. They would be labelled derisively: too loud, too disruptive, too intense, too sensitive, too wild, too rebellious, too much. This sensitive child's utter inability to conform to their tribe's dysfunctional silence would render them a pariah, a black sheep and, I believe in so many cases, laid the foundation for addiction, abusive relationships, depression or suicidal tendencies.

Perhaps society was mistaken in their handling of these children. Perhaps instead of crushing their spirit to toughen them up, shut them up, bottle them up, they should have been nurtured and comforted and helped to navigate the intensity of their inner world. But perhaps these were the new prophets our broken world was begging for? Perhaps my own sensitivity and all those who went before me are in precisely the right era at the right moment, waiting to take centre stage.

These kinds of musings were the fairgrounds inside my head. I whiled away the days and nights pondering all the fantastical ways life could uplift and terrify, delight and amuse, entertain and bewilder us. These kinds of thoughts could only be shared with a few people, like my friend Kate. We could talk through a life problem like a couple of wizened old therapists, drilling down into the minutiae of every plausible motivation or potential outcome. Kate looked like Malibu Barbie, and her deeply insightful and intelligent expression would often take people by surprise, (which I thought to be a sad commentary about stereotypical expectations).

I had never considered myself to be a deep thinker, I was just surprised that other people weren't too. It had taken me until my mid-life to understand that how we perceive other people is measured by our own yardstick of values. If we are honest, we assume others to be the same, if we are kind, we assume others will be too. The same is the case if we are conniving, deceitful, generous, thoughtful, caring, meticulous, moral or righteous. We have expectations of others based on our own inner benchmarks of what we know to be true.

My mid-life had offered me the opportunity to become more like myself. My tragedies had paradoxically made me calmer. I was more precise about my boundaries. Less afraid to be vulnerable. More honest, but my candour was tempered with deeper kindness. I was gentler with myself and consequently with others. And my sensitivity would be my greatest gift.

Chapter 20

WORKOUT WEAR

Once Everleigh had left for England I was at a bit of a loose end. When she was home I had to focus my thoughts, attention and energy on her and her routine. Without her cheery little self to cater to I was alone with the weight of the two possibilities that continued to worry me — jail and indigency. Through years of living in the unpredictability and uncertainty of freelancing I knew that one of the best antidotes to fear of the unknown is to establish a routine.

Part of that routine and one of my lifesaving practices to keep balanced and feel grounded was to go to the gym. Our building had a small gym across the hall from our unit, requiring minimal effort to get there and therefore no room for excuses not to go. My contraption of choice of the small variety of cardio equipment was the elliptical machine; its rhythmic motion could lull me out of almost any frenzied state.

The gym was a small grey room with three large windows overlooking the atrium. It was filled with a decent but basic assortment of equipment and allowed no more than five people to be active all at once. It was always freezing when I walked in, but once I had cranked my music and blasted a few rounds of The Foo Fighters I would peel off my zip-up Lycra jacket and appreciate the sub-zero conditions. I worked out mid-afternoon, and typically the gym was empty — which I was glad for because at times I couldn't hold it together and as my feet would whirl around so would my thoughts, tears silently streaming down my face.

It was a Wednesday afternoon in July and I had just finished a decent workout. My skin was acceptably sweaty and I was in need of a shower. One of the small luxuries in life I always permitted was good-smelling soap. I could spend hours in my favourite home store in the soap aisle, surreptitiously unscrewing the tops of the liquid soaps and smelling them with reckless abandon. My favourites were anything citrus, second would be peppermint or lavender, but anything sweet, or with vanilla or cinnamon would be rejected as if I'd been punched in the face. I had lathered up my lemon and bergamot soap when the palm of my right hand hit a hard lump in my left breast. I froze. It was an unmistakable lump. But I had already experienced a lump in my early thirties, right after the gambling. It had proven to be a cyst, and this would likely turn out to be the same.

Nonetheless, I got dressed and sat quietly on the edge of my bed. I knew that the smart thing to do would be to call Dr Goldstein's office to get it checked out. I padded down the stairs and told Jesse. He was quiet for a beat and then did what Jesse does, tackles a problem head-on and told me to call the doctor's office. I made the call right away, before I had time to think it over or rationalize it away. My appointment was for Friday afternoon.

Jesse drove me to Dr Goldstein's office and dealt with the carousel parking lot while I went to check in. Dr Goldstein was on vacation and his colleague Dr Catherine Taylor was standing in. Jesse and I crowded into Dr Taylor's office as she poked and prodded and concluded that she would have to stick a needle into the area, extract the fluid and send it to a lab. I was glad that Jesse wasn't in the slightest bit uneasy around any medical procedures, but he winced at the needle that was poking around for what felt like an eternity. Dr Taylor was a pretty, petite woman with a calm and benign demeanour and tried her best to assure me and apologize at the same time. I was Dr Goldstein's patient, and she would be ordering up a barrage of testing just to be sure this was nothing to be concerned about. Dr Goldstein was revered in medical circles, and I knew that Dr Taylor would be covering all bases simply because I was his patient.

We left the office and I felt that at least I had taken control of another potentially terrifying outcome. I had faced uncertainty like Joan of Arc, armoured up and looked fear square in the face. This was not going to become a monster in the closet, a festering dark unknown.

Dr Taylor had told us the lab results would take about a week but had scheduled an ultrasound and a mammogram in the meantime. I was to go back to the hospital where Dr Goldstien was now chief of family medicine and where I had delivered Everleigh by emergency c-section. It seemed my whole life I had crashed into one emergency after another, all of it seeming to be beyond my control.

Jesse drove me to the hospital for each appointment, I was grateful for his attention and compassion for the fear I was experiencing. I valued it so much more than just a drive. It was evidence of his evolution. It was Jesse opting to show his support instead of reverting to what he had done previously, look for a logical solution. Previously, he would have said, "It doesn't take two of us to go to the hospital, it makes more sense for me to stay here and clean up."

I had teased him and been annoyed with his logical conclusions at times. I called him Sergeant Sensible. His formerly mission-driven brain wouldn't allow for the time-wasting exercises of bonding, or as I had seen it, being supportive simply by being there.

The hospital was a large urban facility that serviced the northern corridor of the city. It had an excellent reputation and had just been voted in the top three hospitals in the country by Newsweek magazine. It was also under construction, and a patchwork of sleek pristine glass and white smooth lines interspersed with plywood walls and flooring and temporary paper signage. The maze of clinics and check-in desks was scattered illogically on the first floor. We wandered about the futuristic gleaming new hallways, periodically stumbling on the plywood flooring.

When we finally located The Breast Clinic, we settled into the padded blue chairs configured in a square, and I congratulated myself for making the decision to wear trousers. The feeble cotton gowns with even feebler ties were awkwardly placed at the back, I was glad to be wearing something underneath.

There were two visits to this waiting room that week, and each contained plenty of poking, prodding, squeezing and pressing. I had developed a substantial bruise where Dr Taylor had inserted the needle, and the mammogram, as a result, was no picnic. I would do what I had taught myself to do in times of anxiety, I would "zoom out", or slap my attention on something innocuous, the way the machines whirred, or the colour of paint on the walls, or the freezing cold exam rooms and the goosebumps on my arms.

It was a week of distressing testing that had left me feeling vulnerable and anxious. Jesse and I had decided to break our routine and take our neighbour Eva up on her offer to visit her lake house, about two-and-a-half hours outside of the city. We needed to shake off the latest torrent of worry in a place where nature in her majestic artistry could calm our nerves and help soothe the ever-present state of anxiety we were holding at bay.

Chapter 21

SILK DRESSES

The lake house, like Eva's apartment in the city, was crammed with breath-taking and arresting art pieces, from an enormous, exquisite, black-covered, all-white paged pop-up book to a ten-foot-tall oil painting of an astronaut. My artist's soul would jump up and down like an excited toddler every time they added to their collection. Eva's late husband Paul had collected art and Eva had often directed which pieces to buy. Their homes were constructed around the collections and rivalled any self-respecting gallery.

The lake house faced gleaming Lake Ontario, and on sunny days it was bathed in dancing fragments of light, bouncing gleefully off the water's surface. It was an early 2000's back-split with manicured lawns leading down to a large deck with a bunkie that housed the bar and newly renovated bedroom. The serene and secluded little hideaway had the ability to cast a Rip Van Winkle spell and lull its guests into a deep restorative sleep. Huge trees towered over the pathway to the deck and provided a welcome canopy from the sun. The lake offered a constant gentle whisper of a breeze and would soothe its visitors into quietude. It was an idyllic spot, and we were so grateful to be there.

Eva was in her late sixties and suffered from MS. She had also survived a stroke some years before, rendering her already tenuous hold on life even more precarious. Her husband had died suddenly of a heart attack five days after

Jesse's incident. Given Eva's multitudinous health issues and frail physical being, we had all been shocked to lose Paul first.

Although Paul had left Eva with substantial financial means, her memory and physical movement were impaired from the stroke and she needed pragmatic help. Paul had been the logistical officer of their lives. He had taken care of everything — the cooking, the groceries, the appointments, the laundry, all of it. Eva was like a beautiful Italian silk dress without her tuxedoed companion.

We adored Eva and wanted her to feel like she could depend on us now that Paul was gone. Jesse took great pleasure in doing handyman jobs and making sure her environment was safe and functional for her. I would make sure she ate well and didn't rely entirely on a diet of red wine and peanuts. We had the kind of relationship that we could poke fun at each other affectionately and we could buckle up with laughter at the most inane things. She was an artist and interior designer with a colourful past and a hippie soul. We could paint our conversations together with freedom from judgment, sometimes lavishing on thick, gooey rhetoric, sometimes splashing an insouciant but wildly funny jab at our misfortunes. She was my technicolour soul sister, even though we had twenty years between us.

Eva was always delighted to see us. We knew how to be good house guests and we always came prepared with everything we would need to unwind at her oasis. Our apartments in the city had no gardens, so Jesse would relish the time spent outside pruning, trimming, weeding, chopping, it was his therapy and Eva appreciated his brute strength and meticulous attention to each task. I would keep us in supply of heaping plates of food and a constant stream of beverages with profusions of ice. The days we would spend together would be a reprieve for all of us. We would indulge in the hot weather, endless platters of delectable food, copious amounts of gin and tonic and we would bask in the delight of each other's company.

It was around 10 a.m. when my phone rang. We were sitting on the upper deck with coffees in hand, already trying to out-manoeuvre the heat of the July sun. It was Dr Goldstein's office with the lab results. The fluid that had been aspirated from the lump was benign. It was a cyst. I hung up the phone and closed my eyes. I had a moment of solace, and for a brief, illusory time the torture of Jesse ending up in jail, the struggle for Everleigh's schooling, the crushing financial debt and the looming possibility of cancer had all left the stage.

Just a few weeks after those glorious days, however, Joan of Arc, my Navy-Blue Angel and Sigourney Weaver would all be forced to convene in my imagination, preparing a battle plan to face a monstrous antagonist. Lurking in the shadows, hands wringing, beady eyes set upon me, was an enemy that would take every whit of mental fortitude to defeat. I would soon declare war against this beast, and I would be in for the battle of my life.

Chapter 22

COUNTRY CLOTHES

Jesse and I had headed back to the city and almost as soon as we arrived decided to leave again to visit his brother and his wife. They lived two hours west in the countryside just beyond Niagara Falls. Without Everleigh or any kind of routine we had become even more spontaneous and nomadic. I always appreciated that we both could be comfortable just going with the flow, that neither of us had to live by a schedule. I supposed that at our core we knew that we could always figure it out, and on a grander scale, we knew that we were survivors. We had developed a level of confidence about our ability to navigate the unknown.

We were both risk takers in our own ways, and subscribing to the status quo of a conventional life didn't suit either of us. The way we lived and decisions we made had caused consternation for some members of Jesse's family, however-er. They valued a steady job with benefits, simple pleasures and modest dreams. It isn't that we didn't value those things; in fact I had been envious of their ability to be completely satisfied with what appeared to me as mediocrity. Or perhaps it was more that I had become accustomed to a dysfunctional level of drama in my life and from that perspective, anything less than big and intense appeared boring. Regardless, lower aspirations had distinct benefits, and those with them seemed enviably content and fulfilled.

Perhaps I was destined for a higher threshold of unease by virtue of having nor-malized a certain level of unpredictable disorder. But what the hell was "normal" anyway? If a child lives in an abusive home, without considered intervention they seek out abusive relationships, they gravitate towards what they know, what's familiar. To them it's normal. All our experiences point us towards our own unique definition of normal, which is why the word itself is confoundingly inaccurate in describing a unified, middle-of-the-road perspective.

I often wished I could shut off my "big dreams" valve that left me in a constant state of yearning. It was another aspect of myself that I would have to wrestle to the ground and interrogate, but at least I was moving past my compulsion to justify myself and instead embrace my resistance to conform. Middle age had brought me that gift, whereas Jesse had always been content that he simply wasn't wired the same way as most of his family and offered no explanations or apologies. Even when it appeared our lives had gone up in flames, we both knew that for us, living on life's knife edge was a better alterna-tive than a five-by-five office cubicle, fish and chips every Tuesday and a beige coloured house in the 'burbs.

Jesse and I had fundamentally the same values, but our perspective on life and our way of processing information was radically different. I had once heard Esther Perel, a famous psychotherapist, describe two very different ways of thinking as "I am billiards, he is ping-pong" and had laughed at the profound descriptive accuracy of the statement. That was precisely the way that Jesse and I thought about everything. I would evaluate every possible angle on the table, sometimes being able to see the shot with immense clarity, other times getting lost in the possibilities. Jesse would just hammer back a thought like it was the fastest and only option for a result. I valued complexity and savoured conversa-tions that would challenge me to think about things from multiple angles. Jesse valued the most simplistic and direct route to exchange information.

Packing up for road trips would be a perfect demonstration of our billiards versus ping-pong mentality. I would write lists and put post-it notes on everything that was "incomplete"; if the shoe bag was missing a pair of flip-flops I would gleefully slap a post-it note on the bag that read "add J's flip-flops". I tended to organise our clothing requirements for trips like I would organise wardrobe for a gig. I'd consider the access to food, medical supplies, entertainment and weather forecasts. I would pack methodically and meticulously and at times it sent Jesse over the edge. He would cram his pillow and some socks and underwear in his overnight bag and be done with it. But gradually we both gravitated slightly more toward the other. I had learned that we could always find a solution should an item be forgotten, and he had acquiesced to my relentless preparation, coming to appreciate the benefits of having everything we needed in ready order. It was one of the many ways that we had influenced each other for the better.

At this point we had been together for fourteen years and had moved well beyond the romantic phase of our love story. We were in a more mature phase of relationship, where our idiosyncrasies would become what made us excellent teammates. We were learning that these oppositional ways of looking at the world could be complementary rather than a source of conflict.

We loved spending time at Jesse's brother's house. Shane and Violet enjoyed a quiet life in the country with their two oversized loveable rescue dogs and two elusive cats. Violet and I could laugh easily together and gossip over television shows we both enjoyed. She had a penchant for all things British and we were always pinging messages back and forth, "did you watch the latest Call the Midwife or Killing Eve?" She was an affable, down-to-earth woman of exceptional beauty who appreciated her lot in life, although I had always suspected that her alter ego was a Hollywood siren who longed for a bigger existence.

Shane had a ridiculously quick wit and a sense of humour I adored. Which wasn't always an easy connection point for a Brit and a Canadian. The cultural humour was often radically different, and the dry sarcastic banter of a Brit could be easily misconstrued as rude and superior. But Shane was equally sarcastic, and his kind nature would typically steer him clear of flirting on the edge of meanness. On occasion we would run into conflict but had always been able to duke it out, in much the same way two siblings would.

On the Sunday afternoon we were all gearing up for a ramble in the fields with our dogs. A motley crew comprising our shaggy five-pound Chorkie named Jet; Shane and Violet's Tig, a three-legged mutt from war-torn Iran; and Blue, a lolloping German Shepherd cross with hip dysplasia. Our fur-babies were an immense source of love and healing for all of us and we were all sickeningly doting over them.

As I ran down the stairs to collect my shoes, I heard my phone ring. I swung around to run back up and grab it from the hall table. As I picked it up it went dead. The number was from the hospital. Why would they be calling me on a Sunday afternoon?

As the dogs whipped about the long grass, diving in between us as we strolled across the fields, I mentioned the call to Violet. In true character, wanting me to feel better, she quickly dismissed it and assured me it would be nothing. But there was something radically unconvincing about her tone. My mind began to tailspin. Why Sunday? Why wouldn't they leave a message? Was it the kind of news they couldn't leave in a voicemail, or the kind of news not worth leaving a message for?

On Monday morning I would find out.

PART II:
THE FRAGMENTS

'Life-shattering news' – it's an explosion of information that destroys order, predictability, security and a sense of wellbeing.

Chapter 23

BEDSHEETS

At 9 a.m. my phone rang from Dr Goldstein's office.

"Good morning, Rachel, I just wanted to let you know I'm back from vacation and have been reading Dr Taylor's report. I tried to give you a call yesterday from the hospital, but I didn't get an answer."

We exchanged some pleasantries before he continued.

"Anyway, Catherine was exactly right to order up the ultrasound and the mammogram, it was what I would have done had I been here. Listen, I'm not calling you to tell you there's anything wrong, I'm calling you to tell you we need more information. Okay?"

Dr Goldstein had an incredible way of offering firm reassurance and I needed it as the cortisol began to rise. I could feel my throat begin to close and my heart begin to hammer.

"So here's what we're going to do. I'm making an appointment at the hospital for a biopsy. Can you get there on Friday of this week?"

"Yes, absolutely."

"Good. And Rachel, whatever this is, we'll get you through it. Okay?"

His words echoed through my head. I was overwhelmed by his kind reassurance and at the same time consumed by the possibility of what may lie ahead. I was in danger of letting my fears coagulate into thoughts and if I allowed that to happen, I would give unmitigated access to every stress hormone clawing at my insides. I hung up the phone, needing Jesse to ping-pong my feelings into order.

On Friday morning we were back in the hospital. The needle and discomfort of the first appointment kept popping onto the screen of my mind and the palms of my hands would begin to sweat. As I sat in the waiting room, draped in the hospital gown that had all the style of a bedsheet, I tried to distract myself from the impending procedure by considering ways I would reinvent the gowns. What fabric would I use, where would the closures be, how would they fasten, what colours should they be, how would I accommodate all the different shapes and sizes of the human body? I would silk-screen inspirational messages across the back and make them all different colours so patients could choose their favourite. I would make them from bamboo, which was extremely soft, eco-friendly, durable and had antibacterial properties. I would make the ties bigger and much easier to reach and I would keep a stack of blankets beside the gowns so that patients wouldn't freeze their asses off in the waiting rooms. I would allow as many small comforts and choices to a patient as I could imagine the economic and pragmatic constraints of a busy hospital would allow.

Jesse sat beside me with his traveling coffee mug and a rolled-up copy of Popular Mechanics shoved into his pocket. He was equipped to hunker down for the long haul and I was grateful to have his steady, imperturbable presence at my side.

"Rachel Love?" announced one of the nursing staff.

I jumped to my feet and followed the neatly groomed nurse down the hallway and into one of the exam rooms. They were small, well-organized spaces equipped with ultrasound machines, a specialized bed for the patients and fitted cupboards to house all the supplies. The soft, dimmable lighting was akin to an elegant spa treatment room. The images on the ultrasound are better viewed in low light, but the side effect was the calming atmosphere it inadvertently created.

The nurse was considerate about my comfort, offering towels to prop up my arm more easily. She also didn't leave my body unnecessarily exposed, which is tremendously meaningful when feeling so vulnerable. These small, attentive actions helped calm my frenzied thoughts. It was in the waiting rooms that I felt the most tension and where my anxiety would run amok. Once I was situated in the exam room I was more focused on the task at hand.

The nurse left to fetch the doctor and I lay on the bed trying not to be squeamish over the needles I knew would soon be puncturing my left breast. I was relieved when the female doctor entered the room with a smile and a reassuring tone. I was also thankful that this time they would be freezing the area, as the tissue is retrieved for biopsy with a long needle-like contraption that cuts chunks out of the suspected area. I tried to stay focused on the comfort of the bed, the expertise of the doctor and nurse and the magnificence of modern medicine.

It was forty-five minutes of what the doctor described as a "marathon biopsy". They extracted five samples from three different sites. During the procedure the doctor had made a comment to the nurse about one of the sites and needing samples from a "suspected area". I couldn't remember her precise wording, but her language was slightly cryptic and oblique. It was the same type of conversational framework Jesse and I would use if we were trying to have a private conversation but Everleigh was within earshot.

We left the hospital, and once we had reached the privacy of our car I allowed myself to cry. It had always been immensely hard to allow myself to cry openly. I wondered if it was a product of my stiff-upper-lip cultural upbringing, or if never seeing my parents cry made it unacceptable, or if I had put so much pressure on myself to always keep it together I had simply tried to squelch the impulse. Why did we always say "I'm sorry" when crying openly in company? What exactly were we apologising for? An open expression of a perfectly normal emotion, appropriately expressed? Why were we so unaccepting, so ashamed, so apologetic of tears? The visceral relief of letting tears flow should surely be something we encouraged? I made a new bargain with myself. I would give permission to my body to release its stress and if that meant I had to cry, then so be it. If it meant evoking judgment, then so be it. We all needed permission to let go, so I would begin to blaze the trail for myself. What I hoped for was that no one would leap to their feet and offer an awkward hug. I wanted to be left untouched.

The next day when I looked in the mirror, I was stunned to see my entire left breast a kaleidoscope of green and blue bruises. The image was shocking and disturbing, a metaphor for the violence that was happening within my chest, right beside my heart.

Chapter 24

WHITE LAB COATS

Every time my phone lit up with the hospital name onscreen I could feel my heart leap and the chemistry of fear would rip through me. Between that and the periodic calls from Jesse's lawyer, I was sure that if I couldn't find a way to ride out the chain reaction of my fight-or-flight response, I'd be in cardiac arrest any moment.

The hospital called at the beginning of the week with an appointment for that Thursday, August 8th, 2019. My brain went into overdrive. Why would they bring us in for results unless they weren't good? But right after that call, Jesse was on the phone with a colleague who suggested that the only way the hospital could bill for time would be to have the patient present. Whether accurate or not, I was content to accept that as the truth.

Back in the room with the padded blue chairs, we waited. I was draped in the bedsheet gown. Jesse was beginning to pace. Our appointment to see Dr McDonald was forty-five minutes late. Jesse's military-minded timekeeping did not tolerate such deviations from the schedule. Besides, the parking was costing us money we didn't have. The tension was rising, and Jesse was making an already excruciating wait even worse. I called him on it.

"You know, this is hard. I know you're stressed and so am I. Can you please settle down, because I'm feeling your anxiety as well as my own. I need you to engage that military training where you know what to do under pressure and just get your shit together. Please."

Speaking my truth clearly and calmly had become much easier over the previous few months. Jesse was less volatile, less reactive and defensive, and would listen and respond with empathy and compassion. I had become less angry in response and made my requests with a soupçon of humour, offering a Cheshire Cat grin after my delivery. It was my way of easing into this new age of communication between us.

"By the way, Jesse, if this goes south, I need you to stay focused and find out what comes next, ok? I imagine my brain will be scrambled and I'll have a thousand questions I won't be able to access in the moment."

He nodded and I knew he would be able to follow through. He was one of a few people I knew who was extremely capable in a crisis, a painfully paradoxical fact given he had generated such anarchy.

We had sat squirming in the waiting room for almost an hour, when finally we were called into an exam room. This room was different from the others. It was brightly lit with a standard issue exam bench and a couple of chairs facing the doctor's desk. Dr McDonald was a woman in her fifties. Her short grey hair and black-rimmed spectacles gave her immediate gravitas. The lapels of her white lab coat were decorated with a multitude of enamel pins that in short quippy remarks expressed recognition or gratitude. Their presence told me an immediate and important story, that this was a well-loved, experienced doctor. When she spoke it was even more apparent. After a brief introduction she asked to examine me. I hopped up on the bench and could see Jesse fighting his urge to demand she get to the point.

"Oh gosh, you're quite bruised up. From the biopsy I suppose?"

I appreciated her sympathy and gentle touch as she pushed and prodded my beaten body. There was silence as I covered up and made my way back to the seat beside Jesse. Dr McDonald took a breath and said softly,

"It is breast cancer."

Chapter 25

SCRUBS

Jesse was the first to speak after an eternal silence and all he could say was, "Wow. I wasn't expecting that."

After swirling around in an airless few minutes, the prophetic words I'd spoken in the waiting room asking him to pay attention if things went south had landed on him like a hand grenade. He launched into a round of rapid-fire questions:

"What happens now?"

"Will you be our doctor?"

"How bad is it?"

"When will you do surgery?"

Dr McDonald assured us that we would be seeing a lot more of her and she would be with us throughout the process. We would begin with a few more rounds of testing, a bone scan, an MRI and a CT scan.

It hadn't occurred to me until weeks down the line that these tests were trying to determine the extent of the cancer. I was a robot under instruction at that moment and had no bandwidth to think beyond what was happening immediately.

We were gently ushered into a quiet room next door where a new version of my Navy-Blue Angel greeted us. But this time, she was a more mature, blond-haired woman and dressed in scrubs. She wore a name tag that read, "Kim Wegman". She closed the door behind us, and before we sat down she grasped me tenderly by the shoulders and looked me squarely in the eye.

"I can tell by the look on your faces," she began, "that you have just been given this news. I'm going to give you a lot of information here and you won't remember any of it. But I want you to remember this," she paused for a beat and slowed right down for the words to infiltrate. "This is a treatable condition."

Her eyes didn't move away until she could acknowledge that I had registered what she had said. My eyes began to well up, I was overwhelmed and her kind reassurance had pierced the shockwave. She had already reached for a box of Kleenex.

We all took a seat in the quiet little carpeted office. Its blue-trimmed beige furniture was carefully arranged around a central circular table. I wondered if the choice of a round table was a statement of inclusiveness, where there was no power seat, no distinction of status. Kim produced a stack of brochures and booklets and one by one pushed them across the table with an explanation of their purpose. As she had predicted, I don't remember anything she said.

Jesse and I drifted out of the hospital into the startling glare of the Canadian sun. Our bodies moved zombie-like, passing through the milky haze of the parking lot. We were silent until we reached the car and quietly considered who we would call first. Jesse's dad Billy would be the one most able to handle this. He would be calm and wouldn't further dramatize an already surreal moment.

Billy's cheery tone filled the cabin as we cruised into the ever-present wall of traffic on the highway. He rambled a little, telling us of the yearly visit from his cousin, the daily triumphs and frustrations of farm life and neither of us wanted to interrupt. I was grateful for the injection of normalcy into our shattered reality. But his words would come to an abrupt halt after we delivered the news. We could hear his wife, Jesse's stepmother, yelling in the background, "NO! NO! Oh, God NOOOO!"

It was strangely soothing, someone else willing to holler at the injustice on my behalf, willing to rage at the Universe, at God, at random shit luck. Having someone in my corner was so comforting.

With each round of calls, every family member reacted in a way that was precisely as I would have scripted it. As if the most dominant traits of their personalities were condensed into a single reaction. Violet cried and offered anything she was able, Shane cracked some welcome warm-hearted jokes, my mother-in-law and her husband emanated empathy and promises of help.

The overflow of emotion from this small family circle was all I could manage to take in. I wanted everyone to be like Kim, my navigation nurse: steady, reassuring, optimistic, pragmatic. But that was ridiculous. Everyone was going to have their own emotions and I would just have to learn not to absorb it all. I would have to build a bubble around myself and not let their fear in.

Jesse and I considered how we should tell Everleigh. She was with my parents and their response would imprint on her sensitive little soul. I couldn't bring myself to unleash such a wild and untameable monster into their technicolour universe.

"I can't do it, Jesse. I can't tell them. They're having a lovely holiday together. I can't. But then again, I don't want everyone else to know before they do …"

I had no answers, so decided to be silent and wait for the arrival of Joan, Sigourney, and my Navy-Blue Angel. Somehow, an almighty warrior-woman spirit was going to surge through me and I would make the call. But not now. This car ride home was already excruciatingly intense. I would need time to settle into the news, allow the fear to pass through me and land in the greener pastures of acceptance. Jesus, Mary and Joseph, when was that likely to happen?!

The thought of telling my parents was unbearable. All they had heard of late was bad news. I knew my Mum's heart would break and I couldn't bear the weight of watching it happen.

My mother had suffered some immense struggles. A traumatic childhood had haunted her and cemented her internal wiring to be in an almost constant state of fight, flight or collapse. She had worked hard to undo the damage, but without a steady stream of love and support her default response would always be fear-based, no matter how trivial or catastrophic the problem. She could get quickly overwhelmed by life and this was big. I imagined how I would be if Everleigh told me she had cancer. I didn't think I'd be able to get off the floor, and I didn't have to contend with the handicap of years of terror dictating my response.

We were wired to face trauma in our own unique ways. I would charge, hell-fury, into it, she would collapse. We were both products of our history and our personalities, each default mechanism a necessary method of surviving our circumstances.

Although they were always my bedrock of support, both my folks had a tendency of catastrophising at times. My mother simply was unable to cope and could dip into a foggy, numbed-out haze, and my dad could spin almost any news into a cautionary tale. You could tell him you'd won the lottery and before you know it he'd have whipped up a spreadsheet on lottery winners that ended up bankrupt and alone. He was very British and very much a product of his generation; side-step the messy emotional bits, examine the facts, collect the data and then get on with it. His questions could be satiated only by drilling into the minutiae of every aspect of the problem. This being said, my dad would be okay but my mother would be swept away, an unmooring I just couldn't face until I could gather my wits. I would have to coach them, assure them I was in good hands. I would have to be Kim.

Chapter 26

PACKED SUITCASE

Jesse's dad Billy had told us we could drive up to see them. The sprawling acres of the farm and serene and soothing walking trails would help us anchor ourselves. Billy and his wife, Ellen, would offer us the sage wisdom of people who lived off the land and the knowing of those who'd earned their scars. They were people I loved deeply, people I felt safe with, people I knew would hold us up. We needed to be in their presence even when there was nothing they could do to change anything.

We trudged into the farmhouse and into Billy's open receiving arms. He was a towering man of well over six feet with limbs that extended forever. His hugs were always heartfelt and sincere. Ellen would describe herself as socially awkward and people-avoidant with hermit-like tendencies. She would sooner stick a fork in her eye than have to engage in a body-to-body embrace. Yet she held me in her arms for the first time in fourteen years, voluntarily. It was a gesture that almost took my knees out from under me. The welcome hearts of these people and this place was already blooming through us, gently cascading through this latest incarnation of terror.

We sat that evening surrounded by Billy and Ellen, the big skies of the Canadian countryside, our scruffy little fur ball of a dog and Sydney, the farm's titanic yellow lab. The playfulness of the dogs, the clouds drifting overhead, the warmth of this family, had suddenly become intensely precious. What if this was it? What if I would never reach fifty? What if I would suffer like my friend Michelle, who died a horrible cancerous death last year, leaving her two young children motherless and husband widowed? What if I was dead and Jesse was in jail? Everleigh would essentially be orphaned overnight. "What if" — the smallest words that lead in only one direction, to an inevitable island of self-torture. I sat gazing into the wide-open space and decided I wouldn't be getting on that particular train. I would redirect every thought deliberately, consciously, away from disaster and into hope. I wouldn't allow fear to reign over my inner dialogue; I would seize control of my own story and I would sit on the thorny throne of faith.

The farm was a bustling place during the summer and we were always mindful about staying out of the way. An entire year's income would be made in a few short weeks, creating a vacuum of immense pressure with no room for error and certainly no time for guests. Besides, I wanted to witness life as normal, I wanted everything to move at the same pace it always had, with the same grievances and joys of everyday living.

We decided to retreat even further into the Canadian countryside and visit Jesse's Uncle Ben at his island cottage. The cottage where generations of his family had summered every year. Where Shane and Jesse had learned to swim, to fish, to camp, to build fires, drive boats, water ski, make s'mores and in their adult years where they could dump their problems at the opposite shore and ride across the river to their sacred place.

Before we left, I would make that call to my parents. Jesse stayed by my side. It went exactly as I'd predicted. I had gathered enough strength to be Kim and had offered my best reassurances, delivering the news in the most upbeat, optimistic tone I could manage. But I watched my mother drift away and my father attempt to wrestle the shock into a logical place. When he had recovered enough to ask a steady stream of questions, I realized he hadn't heard anything

I'd said beyond "cancer". I knew there would be sleepless nights and intense waves of anxiety to come. I desperately wanted to spare them, but there was no easy way through this inferno. We collectively decided not to tell Everleigh. She could stay in her happy little nine-year-old's bubble, for now.

Chapter 27

SWIMSUITS

Jesse's uncle Ben was a trim, sinewy man in his fifties. His tanned skin told tale of his love of the outdoors. Like all of Jesse's extended family he was warm and welcoming, but as the baby of his mother's siblings Ben was more of a free spirit. A little less bound by the quiet conservative restraints the others operated within. Ben was a cross fit enthusiast and his capable physicality allowed him to indulge his thrill-seeking tendencies. He and Jesse had built fond memories around their mutual love of pushing their physical boundaries. But Ben, being the more senior, was more sensible and less reckless in his older years, and his calming influence on Jesse was something I deeply appreciated.

Ben was there to greet us at the dock. His generous hug and kindly manner was more of what we needed. We loaded the little aluminium boat with the obscene amount of baggage Jesse and I had in tow. The island required additional packing — bedding, towels and a ridiculously large fan that both of us had become accustomed to sleeping under. Our little dog was tucked onto Jesse's lap, his nose sniffing the air with joyful curiosity as we sped across the water to the cottage. What was it about leaving shore that allowed us to leave behind some of our burdens?

Jesse and Ben shared a special bond, exactly the type of uncle-nephew relationship you would imagine unfolding in the pages of a 1950s comic book.

They were a couple of Boy Scouts in their own paradise, fetching wood for the evening's campfire, repairing docks and clearing trails, submerging themselves in the chill of the St Lawrence River when the sweat-load had reached its threshold. But before the traditional activities of cottage life unfolded, we sat with Ben for a cold drink and talked freely about my cancer and what would happen next.

Ben was a high school teacher who lived with his partner Debbie in a pretty little historical town not far from Kingston, the once grand capital city of Canada. They were recent empty nesters; their two amazing girls had been their focus for most of their relationship. Now that the girls had gone to university, Ben was at the cottage daily, at least during the summer and autumn months before the top of the river would freeze over.

The next morning Ben arrived characteristically early, coffees in hand. We sat on the rock point taking in the early morning stillness of the river. I loved this time of day. It was like watching the world stretch into being, slowly waking up, lazily easing into life.

Our morning coffee together never lasted long. As with almost everyone in both our families, none of us could sit still when there were tasks at hand. Jesse was in his element, his bare feet gathering the dirt and grit of the island, his skin soaking up the sun and his mind occupied by only what was directly in front of him.

The cottage was in the throes of a major remodelling. Ben had meticulously hammered every nail, cut every plank of wood and schlepped the mountain of building supplies in the little aluminium boat, virtually single-handedly. Jesse's handyman skills would be put to good use and Ben would make the most of an extra set of hands to tackle the jobs that needed some brute force. As they busied themselves with the build I was left alone with my thoughts.

It was not yet 8 a.m. and already it was hot enough to be in a bathing suit and light coverup. I had nothing to do but observe the world around me. A moment that years ago would have terrified me — to be left alone with no distractions. But in this moment, I was different. I had slammed into enough extreme circumstances to know that I would survive. I knew what I needed to do. In the quiet of that moment, I asked the question, "What is this for?" I often formed clear and precise questions in my head and would miraculously expect the answers to drop in. Sometimes I'd experience an immediate return volley, other times an answer would drift into being over time. It was the closest I would ever get to a meditation — ask the question, wait for the answer, breathe and try to stay present.

As if the island was aware of my presence and the fragile hold I had on my well-being, everything around me seemed to be putting on a show. Two cormorants swooped spectacularly into the river, catching their morning fish. Jesse came over to watch, "Wow, you don't see that very often. Actually, I've never seen that before and two of them. Very cool."

The answer suddenly landed on me like it should have been accompanied by a halo of light and jingle of celestial bells. The thoughts formed as if they weren't mine, like the mother of all epiphanies was having a parade in my head. If it had banners, they would read, "Stay in the moment." "This is all you need and all you can control." "It's all going to be okay." "Yes, this show is for YOU." "That's right … just breathe."

Thoughts that are accompanied by an instantaneous deep feeling of ease are the type of thoughts that make me believe that there is an omnipotent, benevolent force at play, rooting for us, whispering to us. A force that is not yet defined by science and grossly misrepresented by religion. The same force that allows life to flourish, that is always leaning towards growth and evolution. A force that aligns people and things in the exact time and space that they require. A force that can't be seen, tasted, smelled or touched, but that can be felt by every cell within us. A force accessible to anyone, at any time, needing no special words or rituals, traditions or ceremonies, prayers or hymns, logic or reason. A force that is simply there for us to engage with should we choose. Waiting for us to notice the signs, to pay attention to the details, to the inspiration that drops into our awareness when we shift ourselves into the zone. The force that meditation gurus speak of, but that I knew had many routes to access. Evident when athletes were playing their sport, when artists brushed paint on a canvas, when musicians played with their whole body, or, when children played, or even dogs, when their heads were thrust out of open car windows. This force of well-being was everywhere, all the time. I had my confirmation and now I would figure out how to tap into it at will.

There was something magical about this little island. It held generations of memories of Jesse's family and after over a decade of my visiting, I too had found myself under its spell and on this occasion, gifted with its wisdom. I would find a way through this fury, and I would begin with right now.

Chapter 28

FLIP-FLOPS

We let the cottage sink into our bones. The water to calm us, the sun to soothe us and nature to entertain us. With the news spreading quickly I made a list of people I wanted to contact. The worry that someone would refer to my condition on social media was never too far from my mind. When I had discovered I was pregnant nine years earlier the news had reached my social media connections by way of an innocent comment from a friend. I wasn't prepared for the inadvertent public announcement and I did not want a similar situation to happen now. I didn't want good friends finding out that I had cancer from a Facebook comment; they deserved to be told by me personally, and I wanted to be the one telling them.

Ben's oldest daughter Caitlin was going to drop by. Jesse's little cousin, who really wasn't so little anymore. A vibrant young woman in her twenties, Caitlin had the family's over-achiever genetics, was as capable physically as all of Jesse's family, and had a deep-hearted kindness and soulful enquiry that I connected with immediately. I adored Caitlin and her little sister Maisie.

Telling people such life-changing news can be exhausting, it takes an emotional toll that's amplified to an excruciating level when the receiver is someone we love. I was consciously keeping my terror at bay, redirecting, moulding, sculpting, manipulating every fearful thought. If I were to witness Caitlin's shock I'd be revving the engine of fear and risked losing my own tenuous grip on hope.

She would be driving for hours before she arrived, so I asked Jesse to call her. It would give her time to process, and I could be spared becoming the sobbing mess I knew I would be if delivering the news to her face to face. There would be too many opportunities to collapse into sadness and fear and I must be Kim. For my own sanity and theirs.

Jesse made the call. I was grateful to be able to lean on him, to relax my grip on containing and controlling life, to let him step up and hold the wheel for a while. I was beginning to feel the turn in our relationship. I stepped away from being his overbearing parent and he, the petulant teenager. It was all beginning to transform.

Caitlin picked up her mum en route to the cottage. Debbie was the embodiment of what it is to be Canadian: fun, friendly, welcoming, down-to-earth and one of my favourite people to spend time with. She and I could laugh hysterically over the most ridiculous things. We would often drag the plastic Adirondack chairs out to the shallow rocky point and allow our feet to dangle in the cold water. Sometimes, if we weren't paying attention, a boat-generated wave would catch us by surprise, leap through the slats in the bottom of the chairs and soak our bums. It would make us laugh hysterically. Or the time Debbie's sun-baked plastic chair had decided it had had enough. Its weakened rear leg snapped in protest and dumped her unceremoniously into the river. She managed to save her cocktail on the way down, which caused us to laugh even harder.

Ben picked them up from shore and when they reached the dock they all deftly transferred themselves and their belongings from the wobbly little boat onto the steady wooden pier-like dock. Canadians were so capable around water. In a country of over two million lakes learning to swim was required, and driving a boat was almost as common as driving a car.

We greeted each other with a warm and sincere hug. I knew I could push my anxiety into submission in the company of these two affable, vibrant women. It didn't take long before the cancer talk was over, food was being prepared and cocktails were flowing. The intensity of my gratitude was sublime, because the chance that I might not get to do this ever again was a very real possibility. The sheer entertainment of such notions must be shoved in a file and placed in an unretrievable corner of my mind.

We slowly made our way back to the city, stopping in to visit a number of Jesse's relatives along the way. Their kindness and compassion seeped into us at every stop. I considered the contrast between the trauma of Jesse's incident and the trauma of this news. When Jesse had blown our lives apart I felt an element of shame as his wife. I could feel the judgment and incredulity of those evaluating our situation: Why would a forty-year-old man be compelled to take magic mushrooms? Why would I stay in such a dysfunctional relationship? Why didn't I have enough self-respect to just leave? Why wouldn't I protect my child and take her away from that monster?

I had been crushed by the weight of what he had done, felt murderous on behalf of his victim and mangled by the consequences. Consequences that were still pending. Consequences that could still leave me without a husband. The memories of the incident and dread of what could still happen drifted like a noxious poison in and out of my daily thoughts. During my sleep my jaw would be clamped so tightly shut my dentist had given me powerful muscle relaxants and noted my gums were receding as a result of the enormous pressure.

But the trauma of cancer had launched me into an arena of compassionate support, where every emotion was catered to, cared for, considered and resourced. This trauma elicited immense kindness from total strangers and caused family and friends to rush into service. This trauma was placated by thoughtful cards and home-baked treats, and that kindness permitted the hot stinging tears of helplessness.

Chapter 29

COFFEE-STAINED SHIRTS

Jesse was driving differently than he had. He drove more slowly. He was more deliberate, more cautious, more thoughtful. I had often thought that the way people drove offered immense insight into their personalities. Were they competitive, aggressive, arrogant, complacent, reckless, careless, inconsiderate? Or were they courteous, thoughtful, calm and aware of the immense responsibility of having passengers in their cars? Did their impatience on the road equate to their impatience with others? Did their competence behind the wheel belie a competence in other skills? I had adjusted my own driving style after a spectacular incident circa 2004.

That summer day, I had been driving out of the city with a girlfriend. We had a fledgling business and had secured an important meeting with a potential mentor and investor. The Don Valley Parkway is a major highway on the east side of the city that winds its way north to south in a three-lane, snake-like configuration. It was always one of my favourite highways. I loved the challenge of its narrower lanes, high speed and twisting roadway. I had always driven a standard vehicle, an unusual choice in North America where most cars had automatic gear shifts. I preferred to control the gears and somehow felt more connected to the car itself. I had a silver Volkswagen Jetta, a VR6 with all the bells and whistles. I loved that car.

It was a gorgeous sunny day. The highway was busy as usual, but it was just after rush hour and we were going north against the traffic heading south into the city. I was situated in the far left lane, the fast lane, cruising well above the speed limit at one-twenty. I entered a long bend just as I had put my coffee cup back into its holder. As I glanced up from the holder, a small white pick-up truck in the lane beside me had taken the bend a little too fast and his vehicle was pushing the edge of his lane and into mine. I had taken in the snapshot of what looked like a near collision and reflexively pulled the wheel to the left. But my wheels were already turned to the right and at that speed I had grossly overcompensated.

In a few seconds we were fishtailing violently in the lane, then as if we were a child's spinning top we began to whip in circles back and forth across the three lanes of the highway. We spun with such ferocity that my arms, still glued to the steering wheel, were criss-crossing wildly over each other. Our coffees, secured in their holders, were spewing their contents through the tiny little holes in the lids with such force that arcs of coffee were hitting the roof then landing on us.

We spun three times across all three lanes, careening within inches of the other vehicles and the barriers on either side of the highway. There was a gigantic MAC truck in the middle lane just behind us and as we spun, its grill came closer and closer like a T-Rex about to have us for lunch. It was the first time I had experienced the peculiar bending of time, like everything was happening in slow-motion while it only took seconds to unfold.

I also experienced an inexplicable calm as we whipped around in circles. I felt what I can only describe as a presence, a knowing, that omnipotent life force breathing us into safety, I knew that we would be okay.

With each spin we watched the grill of the MAC truck appear ominously closer until it seemed inevitable we would end up mangled under its wheels or embedded in its engine. The truck driver slammed on his brakes and sounded his horn, alerting the entire highway of the catastrophe unfolding. The noise of the truck, the smell of burning rubber and an ensuing wall of smoke had descended over the tarmac. We screeched to a spectacular halt smack in the centre of the middle lane, facing the right direction. As if we'd been placed there, as if it had been orchestrated.

We sat incredulous that we had come out unscathed. Not even a scratch on the car to show what we had survived. As the wall of smoke behind us began to settle it revealed hundreds of vehicles at a complete standstill, an instant gridlock of traffic. In front of us, a wide-open highway. It was just us, perfectly situated in the middle lane, as if we were leading the charge into battle. We both let out an audible gasp. I took my car out of fifth gear, put it in first, then eased over to the slow lane and continued the drive.

The driver of the MAC truck pulled up alongside us and gestured to us with hand signals asking if we were ok, and then swiped his hand across his brow as if to wipe away sweat, implying, "Holy crap, that was close!" We pulled off the highway and found the nearest gas station bathroom to get the coffee out of our clothes and hair and to buy a lottery ticket.

Hours later, it occurred to me that I could've killed my passenger or any of the other drivers on the road that day. The thought had made me physically shake, as if someone had taken me by the shoulders and relentlessly jerked me back and forth. The experience would change my driving forever. I would be more in tune with my surroundings, more diligent with my attention and would take the road at a slower speed. It was also a moment I would reflect on often and would marvel that I was alive. It had to be for a purpose, didn't it?

Chapter 30

NAIL POLISH

Back in the city, Jesse and I hit our lives' play button once again. My agent had secured one of the biggest and most challenging jobs of my career and I was scheduled to deliver a large deck of content to two entrepreneurs looking to pivot their fashion business. In between the almost daily hospital visits, I crammed in as much work as I could, knowing my income would grind to a halt soon enough. People assume — I had assumed — that cancer would come riddled with symptoms and changes in energy, but I had no symptoms, no inward or outward evidence that there was anything wrong with me. I was eager to plunge into projects. They offered me welcome distraction and without Everleigh at home it was easier to focus on a demanding schedule.

Jesse and I had found common ground in our vastly different work experiences. Production work and military operations had tremendous commonalities: Mobilization of dozens or hundreds of soldiers or crew into different daily locations, under any weather conditions and within insane time limits. We respected each other's hard-working attitude and always supported the other's efforts.

Our work ethic extended into our home. We worked seamlessly to get a job done and were both meticulous in our execution of a task. It was something we appreciated about each other, at least at this stage in our relationship. I had been too critical in the past, noticing only the incomplete detail, or any minor mistakes. I was quick to point out what didn't meet my exacting standards and forget to mention, or notice, anything good. Jesse had mentioned this on several occasions and eventually the message had sunk in.

I was a product of my past as well as my innate personality and that highly critical voice had been commonplace in my childhood. Like every child, I had internalized the criticism and developed my own intolerant voice. By the time I was a teenager I was filled with self-hatred and my self-esteem had been beaten into submission.

I had observed from a very early age that the way most people lived their lives was profoundly unfulfilling and joyless. Their expectations of happiness were excruciatingly low. The prevailing mentality around work, marriage and parenthood were all matters of duty and obligation rather than sources of joy and fulfilment. I knew there was more to it than daily drudgery and endless random experiences of bad luck. There had to be. Maybe all this lunacy that was unfolding was going to teach me on a level way beyond therapy and my library of self-help books.

I had always believed that when the student is ready the teacher will come, and in my early twenties, as soon as I had earned a pay cheque, I sought out a therapist, believing they would be able to fix me. I was earning seven dollars an hour and paying my therapist a hundred. But I was never going to return to the debilitating depression I had fallen into at seventeen; that was a cost too great.

I stayed in therapy for eight years, most of it participating in small group sessions. It was terrifying at first; I barely spoke for almost six months. I was so disconnected from my emotions I relied upon a cheat sheet of emojis with various expressions to help me identify what I was feeling. Psychological research had always fascinated me and recently I had read about the importance of being able to name our emotions. The mere labelling of them would help diffuse their intensity, a practice coined simply as "name it to tame it". It was within the safety of that small therapy group that I had learned some critical emotional language and developed some basic skills around having tough conversations.

Jesse and I were operating in a new atmosphere. We were softer, kinder, more unified in our grief and in the uncertainty of each day. Our personal burdens were so big we simply compartmentalized them to get through the waking hours. I stayed focused on every possible source of joy and carefully monitored every external influence, not allowing myself to search for breast cancer online or read about the horror stories of other patients and survivors. I closed ranks with the people I trusted and who would be a positive influence. I didn't even want to join any cancer related support groups. I didn't want my identity to become wrapped around this disease, I didn't want to know more about it, and I didn't want to talk about it more than I had to. I didn't want it to consume any more of me than it already had.

Keeping cancer from swallowing me whole was off-set by an outpouring of kindness. Complete strangers generously prepared delicious meals for us and almost daily, cards, flowers and thoughtful gifts streamed through the front door. A fellow freelancer began a fundraising campaign to help with the inevitable financial burden of being sick while self-employed. Friends came armed with everything from wine to nail polish, offering company or beauty treatments. At times it was hard to accept. But I had to learn to accept if I was going to get through this. I would have to take off my inner armour and let the love in.

There is an excruciating time lapse between discovering you have cancer to knowing how bad it is. By the beginning of September I had been tested and evaluated for every possible worst-case scenario. Living in that place of un-known consequences was for me the most challenging part of cancer. It's a mind-fuck thinking that your body could be riddled with cancerous cells, devouring life from the inside. Yet I was one of the luckiest and most privileged patients, already enrolled in a world-class hospital with a crackerjack team of caring and heavily credentialed doctors. Being in such competent, capable hands had kept much of my fear at bay. Each member of my medical team was someone Jesse and I had immediate affection and respect for.

My plastic surgeon Dr Mahoney, who would be performing the reconstruction of my left breast, was a woman I wanted to befriend — a triathlete and the mother of young children, two important details that implied to me that she was a woman of grit and determination. Not only for her athletic ability, but for juggling motherhood and a demanding career. She had an equable, convivial manner and was deeply committed to her patient's well-being and comfort. We had connected with her immediately.

At one appointment she took pains to outline what would happen during my three- to four-hour surgery she would be sharing with Dr McDonald, who would be removing the tumour. She showed me the silicone implant that would be inserted in place of my natural fat and tissues, and took her time to precisely measure and evaluate which implant best matched the other side. As a stylist, I appreciated her meticulous attention to the aesthetic outcome. She asked permission to take some headless photographs and I quipped, "Of course! Anything for your social media feed."

She also assured us that if my left boob was higher than my right, post-surgery, she could tuck and lift the right one to match. At which point I smacked Jesse's arm and said, "Merry Christmas honey!"

Chapter 31

RAGS AND RICHES

By the end of August Everleigh had returned, thankfully with happy memories and two solo flights without incident. In fact, she had loved the experience and happily chatted away to us about her seatmates on her return flight. I had asked for the advice of my navigation nurse about the best way to talk to your kids about cancer. She had sent me some helpful articles that suggested being upfront without drilling down into the details. I knew that Everleigh's insightful and enquiring mind wouldn't tolerate anything less, but I also knew she could be engulfed with fear if we didn't carefully vet the information.

I wanted to control the narrative for her, but knew that the prevalence of cancer would elicit terrifying stories from friends and schoolmates who had lost loved ones to the disease. I told her that there were lots of types of cancer and that I had the type you don't die from. I obviously omitted from going into more detail that at least the odds were in my favour, with a one-in-five fatality rate. I told her about all the incredible doctors I had and that I was being treated at the same hospital she was born. The same hospital she was supposed to be incubated in for two to three months, but because of her strength and the excellent care she received was out of the NICU in ten days. I told her I too had that strength, and these doctors were incredibly experienced and knew exactly what to do. I told her how I thought her life would be impacted after my surgery and chemo and radiation and that Daddy would be spending much more time cooking. Only at that point did she say, "Oh no!"

I assured her, like I assured everyone, that I wasn't afraid because I was in excellent hands. I didn't tell anyone that sometimes at 3 a.m. a terror would lunge at me and grab me by the throat so tightly I thought I might pass out.

My surgery was scheduled for Monday September 9, 2019. We had just spent our annual cousins' weekend at the farm, where all Jesse's cousins and their families gathered for a long weekend of camping. His cousin's wife had made a box of "Mammo-Graham S'mores", a hilarious stack of cookies with a boob-shaped marshmallow squashed between two biscuits.

I loved his family and wondered if they knew how important their presence was in my life. With such a nomadic childhood that consisted of nine schools, over thirty-five moves and living on three continents, the anchor of extended family was something I missed and often yearned for. I had envied parents who had the support of nearby grandparents, or cousins who enjoyed sleepovers and large family vacations. But constant change had provided me with a rich patchwork of experience, and exposure to other cultures had deepened my understanding of the world around me. So much change had made me adaptable and resilient, allowed me to know that I could fit in anywhere, with any crowd. At least that was a perspective I came to well into my thirties. Before that I was too busy trying to fit in, unwittingly compromising my own values in favour of being liked.

As a child I lived with my family in New Delhi for two-and-a-half years. I was almost eleven when we left, old enough to remember the experience. We had a beautiful new house, a driver, cook, nanny, gardener and even a person who washed our clothes. Even the humblest circumstances for foreigners entailed having a servant or two. Servants were status quo for white people, even poor white people.

Right next door to our house was a building site. A family of four lived there, full-time, on the building site — two little kids, Mum and Dad hunkered under a bedraggled makeshift tent. Their kitchen was an open-fire pit, one battered tin pot dangling over the open flames. Our driver, Barret, would take my toddler brother over to visit, drink chai and play with the little boy. He was a couple of years older than my baby brother, probably around four or five and of approximately the same weight. One day my Mum had invited this little boy to come and play with my brother in our sandbox. Bright yellow Tonka trucks and sand toys scattered throughout, my brother "brummmed" the cars up and over the sand hills. All the little boy could do was stand at the edge of the sandbox and watch, awestruck. He had no idea how to play with such toys. It was overwhelming for him, for us, to be staring privilege so blatantly in the face. It was one of dozens of moments that would contribute to my understanding of privilege over the years.

As blonde haired, blue-eyed siblings my brother and I were like art exhibits when we went out in public. It was the late 1970's, and our colouring wasn't commonplace. We would frequently have our hair touched or our cheeks pinched by complete strangers. All well-intended gestures, but nonetheless unnerving for us and for my mother, who would frequently be left holding a wailing toddler having had his cheeks squeezed blood red from acts of impulsive cuteness aggression.

Being a perpetual newcomer, I had plenty of experience being viewed as an outsider, being told I was "different". It was why fitting in had become such an overwhelming tenet of my daily existence. It was, in part, why I had strived so exhaustingly to be liked, to be approved of, to be accepted by every new tribe.

Being an outsider is intrinsically lonely. It had taken decades of rejection and exclusion from friend cliques that had made me so sensitive to anyone new in a neighbourhood, and I would always go out of my way to be friendly. It had also taken me decades to understand the subtleties between fitting in and belonging. When I read some of the work by research professor Brené Brown, she outlined this notion so beautifully. The idea that true acceptance stems from a feeling that you can be authentically yourself and be accepted, rather than trying to be like everyone else in order to fit in. In my late forties I was much more interested in belonging. The days of my performative dog-and-pony show were well behind me. I wish we would celebrate these benchmarks of self-acceptance as we age, instead of being so superficially focused on warding off wrinkles or saggy body parts.

Jesse's family bizarrely consisted of every kind of engineer you could train to be. They were an over-achieving, impressively credentialed group of people it was easy to feel intimidated by. They were also incredibly warm and loving and I felt a deep connection to many of them. I tried not to let that connection be taken for granted and I was careful to acknowledge what I loved, if sometimes I was regarded warily when my compliments were too effusive. But I had found immense joy in the process of looking for the good in people, keeping focused on what I liked and then forming the words to wrap around the feelings of appreciation, almost as if I were paying penance for my formerly critical self and my British influence, never to be too emotive or overly encouraging. I thought it such a ridiculous shame that the best things that are spoken of us are shared at our funerals.

Cancer provides an excellent excuse to speak freely for our love of people if we so choose. And if my days were numbered I was going to take every opportunity to notice the goodness in everyone. I would stop my inner critic in her goose-stepping path and shower her with confetti love hearts. I would forgive more quickly, understand more deeply and make a gargantuan effort to respond with more love and less judgment. Not because I was vying for some kind of humanitarian gold medal, but because my sanity depended on it.

Our psychological tanks filled with the relaxed and happy memories of the weekend, we felt as though we had laid a stable foundation for the day of my surgery. I had a quiet sense of ease with just a ribbon of anxious anticipation. I had sat in the discomfort of both mild and acute anxiety many times in the last few months, and I had learned to treat the feeling as if it was a weather front moving in. I would mindfully step out of the intensity and try to just observe it. I would say things to myself like: "This is interesting, this feeling I'm having right now. I feel some anxiety and that's completely understandable. It's okay to feel like this. It'll pass soon enough. I won't feel this way in a few hours, maybe even a few minutes. In fact, what is actually happening right now in this moment? I'm safe. I'm not alone. I'm not hungry or thirsty or tired. I can breathe more slowly or move about a little to quell this feeling. I got this." The awareness of this inner narrative had become a portal to a host of better coping mechanisms.

A critical intervention I had performed on myself was inspired by the profound words of Viktor Frankl the Austrian psychiatrist, neurologist and philosopher who had survived two Nazi concentration camps and the near obliteration of his family. Frankl had faced despair and adversity the likes of which I would never know, so his words were like gospel to me. He said, "Between stimulus and response there is a space. In that space is our power to choose our response. In our response lies our growth and our freedom." But it wasn't just the practices I had learned in the last few months that had given me some comfort. It was the knowledge that I had an incredible team of doctors and surgeons and that I had Jesse by my side. Jesse 2.0, new and improved, like he had a giant shiny sticker on his forehead.

We settled ourselves into the blue hospital chairs, books in hand, in the hopes we could find distraction in their pages. We waited in three different waiting rooms consecutively, beginning at 7 a.m. for a dye to be injected so my lymph nodes could be easily detected and removed for pathology, the results of which would tell us how far my cancer had spread. Each waiting area inched closer to my surgery, scheduled for 11:45.

Our last tiny waiting area was shared with two fellow cancer patients. I was always the youngest of the group since the average age for breast cancer is sixty-two. One of the patients had lost her hair and was chatting about her experience of radiation being worse than chemo. I bounced my foot uncomfortably and decided to get up and walk up and down the hallway. Mental self-preservation wasn't always convenient.

Jesse and I found two empty chairs at the end of the hall. A thoughtful orderly had handed me a warm blanket and once again I was overcome with gratitude for such tiny considerations. With time stretched out in almost unbearable fragments, we tried our best to engage with our books, but we were like fidgeting preschoolers, unable to get comfortable or settle down. The slight ribbon of anxiety I had felt earlier in the day had become a little more taut as the surgery drew closer and closer but I mostly still felt I was in the driving seat of my emotions.

Finally my name was called and I was walked down into the pre-op room where the anaesthesiologist explained what would be happening. I knew my surgery would take about three or four hours tops and that I should be able to go home right away. But like the rest of my life recently, it wasn't going to go to plan.

Dr Mahoney came in and stood at the end of my bed like she was ready to take on her next triathlon. Her confident, sanguine energy filling the room with propitious expectation.

"Ready?" She asked.

"Only if you are." I replied.

Chapter 32

UNWANTED ACCESSORIES

Somewhere between seven and nine that evening I woke up. I couldn't move. How could I not get up out of bed? I had lost my boob, not my legs. The pain was remarkable and getting up was like trying to scale the side of a collapsing mountain. I buzzed for a nurse, who helped me drag the cumbersome IV into the bathroom, inch by painful inch manoeuvring around my roommate's curtain and past the obstacles of visitors' chairs. My throat was sore and dry from being intubated, and my body felt like it had been tossed around in a life-sized tumble dryer. I had grossly underestimated the impact of the surgery.

I'd had a c-section at the age of thirty-eight and bounced back after a couple of weeks. Perhaps being forty-something really was that much harder to physically recover. I pushed the thought aside; my recovery would be swift, I told myself. But on my way back to the bed I needed to vomit, sending my poor nurse scurrying for a container. As the nausea passed I realized I would need to talk myself into recovery with a little more conviction.

All my belongings were still in a locker somewhere in the hospital, my phone stuffed into one of my pockets. I had no way to contact Jesse and hoped he would show up soon. It was later that evening when he arrived with Everleigh, her little face motionless as she tried to take in all the equipment and assess the impact on her life. She sat gingerly at the edge of my bed and asked if I needed anything. Jesse sat in the little chair beside us then poked her in his fun-loving way,

"Hey Everleigh, tell Mommy what just happened on the highway."

Her face became wildly animated as she told me that as they were about to take the off-ramp to the hospital, they had been talking about the importance of watching your surroundings on the road, and how quickly accidents could happen.

"Then … Mommy, you're not even gonna believe it," she said excitedly. "This car, right in front of us, crashed right into this other car. Like, right in front of us!"

Jesse interjected with a more precise and detailed account of the collision, assuring me the driver looked okay. At least he was within a stone's throw of a great hospital, I thought. I was so grateful for my little family, here beside me, safe and well.

Jesse told me my surgery had taken almost seven hours, that there was an unforeseen complication and that's why I had to stay overnight. My skin had been too thin to accommodate the silicone implant, so Dr Mahoney had had to improvise with a temporary skin expander. The implications were a few more visits to the hospital and another future surgery once my skin had healed. But, "Good news!" he declared, "they did save your nipple. And they removed five tumours."

If it wasn't for the benign cyst that sat prominently just under the surface of my skin, these five festering tumours would never have been discovered. I pondered the idea that the cyst had signposted the way to cancer and I wondered if the cells of my body had a kind of sui generis intelligence, perhaps a consciousness of their own?

My overnight stay in the hospital was interrupted every two hours for a check on my vitals. Shrouded by a flimsy blue curtain, my roommate snored loudly, making sure that sleep was virtually impossible even with my earplugs and headphones covering my ears. I couldn't wait to get out of there.

Chapter 33

PYJAMAS

The following afternoon I was released from the hospital. The week consisted of a monotonous treadmill of lethargic movement from bed to couch to bathroom, perforated by sleepless nights mired in discomfort. I was only able to lie on my back, and had to wear an excruciatingly tight surgical bra round the clock, which initially was like getting into a slingshot. With limited range of motion in my left arm, a cyborg-like tube hanging out of my side and wads of post-surgical dressings across my chest, getting in and out of any clothing was a Sisyphean task. The series of tiny hook-and-eye closures at the front of the sling-shot-bra was an extra-special challenge. Why would anyone design a garment for people post-surgery with the tiniest hardware available?! This was another product I would have to redesign, and it would involve lots of velcro.

I had rounds of meds to take every few hours and by the end of the week I was miserable. I couldn't eat, couldn't sleep and the morphine was wreaking havoc on my bowels. A plastic tube was coming out of my torso just below my armpit, which ended in a small silicone bladder that had to be emptied every few hours. It grossed me out. I wasn't particularly squeamish, but I didn't like watching the contents of my own body dripping into a bag. Thankfully, Jesse was unfazed and went about administering meds and emptying the drain and moving me and my bedding carefully between locations. He was present and attentive and everything I had hoped he would be.

During my week in recovery Daniel had called needing another five thousand dollars for Jesse's defence fund. The news had sunk me into despair. We were broke, I couldn't work and my fear was consuming. My broken body had no strength to overcome anything, so I sat in a heap on the floor and cried. The weight of it all was immense.

I couldn't shake the phone call, or my gut-wrenching sense of doom. A few hours had passed, and I made a conscious effort to consider the moment I was in right then. Nothing had actually changed in my immediate reality.

I went back to the words of Viktor Frankl, "stimulus and response" I needed to find the space in between and observe, rather than react. What was the story I was telling myself? What was contributing to the anxiety that was within my control? I was under the spell of information, which I had allowed to take over my inner world. I had invented a virtual reality of painful consequences that didn't even exist.

The money could be made back. So what if we accrued some debt? We'd pay it off. I constructed a visual reference for myself. I would let this news land on me like a post-it note of information, not a billboard plastered to me with crazy glue. I would let this moment be and then shake free of it. I wouldn't torture myself with superficial positive affirmations, either. Although I felt it was paramount to find something positive to focus upon, that focus could not be at the expense of what I was truly feeling. That was the root of "toxic positivity" – denying painful experiences by glossing over them with a rainbow paintbrush of saccharine platitudes. I would just try to inch my way out of despair and towards something slightly better. I would distract myself from the pain. I would find a movie I wanted to watch. I would find something good to drink. I would get up, and I would move forward.

While Everleigh was at school was when I allowed myself to fall apart. I hadn't wanted her to absorb the burden of such adult concerns; I wanted her childhood to be as carefree as I could make it. She was worried enough about her own little world of struggles in school. If she did catch wind of what was happening, I wanted her to see that no matter how big the struggle, we would figure it out, together, as a team. I wanted her to witness resilience, to know that her parents would tackle whatever they needed to, to keep her safe. I didn't want her to do what I had done as a child, to start on-boarding problems as if they were my responsibility to resolve, to manage, to prop-up, to care, fix and fight for. I didn't want to create a parentified child by not paying attention to just how much she was taking in. I wanted her to be spared from adult complexities, at least until she had done some living and had a fair chance at being a child.

Everleigh was the sweetest nursemaid, fetching me water and smoothies, expertly helping me up from lying down. She had a tiny little frame but had inherited her athletic ability from Jesse and her tenacity from both of us, making her a mighty little hurricane of energy when required. She quickly assessed the best way to assist in leveraging me off the couch, and perfected the technique in a couple of attempts. I knew that if I was going to recover quickly both mentally and physically, I would need to amplify these small triumphs and tender moments. I would need to set my focus on what was working and make a point of remembering the tiny moments of joy.

Chapter 34

PARTY HATS

Nine days after my surgery Everleigh was turning ten. Birthdays were important to me, especially childhood ones. A celebration entirely for one person whose presence in the world was utterly unique. Considering the odds of us being born are at least four hundred trillion to one, I had always thought that most birthdays weren't an accurate reflection of such a mind-blowingly miraculous probability. At the very least, they were a day worthy of a decent cake and a little pomp and ceremony.

I had always been the party planner. Jesse — like virtually every other husband, my girlfriends and I had complained — was seemingly incapable of pulling together all the accoutrements of a noteworthy birthday party. Although I couldn't ever subscribe to lavish three-tiered cakes for two-year olds, or pink-dyed ponies delivering bespoke, designer gifts, I did want Everleigh to be celebrated, to be with her friends and have memories of being cherished and acknowledged. After all, how many birthdays would I get to plan for her?

I knew that if I left it to Jesse, we might have a box of cupcakes from the discount grocery store and a gift or two, possibly wrapped in Christmas paper. There had been a time in our relationship when his gift giving had caused us to fight. A box of very traditional stainless steel cutlery from a website where people could flog their wares, being a more notable Christmas gift. A kitchen mat for my birthday in another year. His track record had been so substandard I had felt panic whenever he handed me a gift. But in recent years, his gift-giving, along with his thoughtfulness, had become pretty spectacular. Still, planning a party would be a responsibility he would despise with a guaranteed outcome of a disappointed kid.

I had a vast network of talented women I could call on and decided I would have to start operating outside of my customary independent, self-sufficient ways and ask for help. When we're raised to value autonomy and our efforts are evaluated in an unyielding meritocracy, asking for help is an unnecessarily uncomfortable, foot-shuffling experience. But I wanted this party for Everleigh, my surgery wouldn't allow me to lift my arm very high and the meds had left me exhausted. I put out the call to two of my friends with impeccable taste and who I knew could work within my shoestring budget.

With a cash injection from her grandparents and on the advice of another mum, I booked a hotel room for Everleigh and four friends. Along with gorgeous, personalized loot bags, the party boasted charming decor, a divine chocolate cake with her name emblazoned on top and a spread of colourful junk food, complete with paper unicorn straws and pretty paper plates.

I could never have imagined that a group of tweens excitedly shrieking about the pool, the bowls of candy and their carefully curated loot bags would be such good medicine. It wasn't just the girls who provided such a welcome respite from our daily distress, it was my girlfriends who showed up. They had coordinated and carefully designed such a special collection of things to create a beautiful memory for Everleigh. I was beginning to understand the vital requirement that cancer demands: to ask for help, then relish in the receiving of it. It was a new magnitude of love that was being handed to me. It was time to practice vulnerability and gratitude on a scale I had never had occasion to access before.

Chapter 35

HOSPITAL GOWNS

As soon as Everleigh's birthday candles were blown out, it seemed, I was back to the hospital for check-ups and more testing. Our near-daily routine became bone scans, CT scans, ultrasounds, echocardiograms, blood work, and needle after needle being stabbed into my body. On September 25th, I met with my oncologist, Dr Thompson, another woman Jesse and I felt immediately comfortable with. Attentive, considerate and self-assured, she was a woman also in her forties, with ten years of oncology experience. As I assessed Dr Thompson, I remembered something a neurologist friend of mine had said, that there's an ideal time for doctors to be practicing. You don't want one who's been around too many years and is not open to new possibilities, but you also don't want a fresh-faced newbie right out of med school. The sweet spot, she had told me, was around seven to ten years post-graduation.

During our first appointment Dr Thompson had outlined all the side effects of chemo: Yes, I would lose my hair. I might have permanent pins and needles in my hands and feet. And yes I would have to make sure I didn't get a cold because infection could kill me. She explained that they would be testing my heart to see if it could withstand the treatment, taking blood every other week to see how much my white cells had depleted, inserting a picc line into my arm for the duration of the treatment (otherwise my veins would collapse if the drug was administered in my arms) and I would have to take a powerful anti-nausea concoction by way of injecting myself in the stomach. Dr Thompson had delivered all the information with an easy-going efficiency that made it sound like everything was going to be just fine. We believed her.

During our appointment I relayed something my oncology surgeon had mentioned to me. "Dr McDonald suggested I ask you about an …" I paused as I read the note on my phone, "Oncotype DX test?"

"Yes, that's right," Dr Thompson replied reassuringly, "I agree with Dr McDonald. It's a test they only perform in California and it'll tell me precisely how effective chemo will be for you, or if you need it at all. I think you're a good candidate for the Oncotype since your numbers sit bang in the middle of low to high risk. But I want you to know, based on the pathology of the five tumours that test is highly unlikely to indicate that you're not going to need chemo. One was very aggressive and there is micro-cell activity in your lymph nodes. So, I'm going to forge ahead with the treatment schedule and I want you to assume we'll be beginning in October. John is our drug administration assistant. He'll give you the additional paperwork to apply for the drug funding and I'd also like to offer you an appointment with a psychiatrist if you'd like that?"

"I'd never miss an opportunity to sit with a shrink."

Dr Thompson smiled and we left her office trying to buoy ourselves up with comments about inane things, as if we hadn't just been told that my immune system was about to be obliterated.

Jesse's life was playing out in tandem, the two of us facing potentially devastating outcomes that would affect us for the rest of our lives. It was hard to fathom the implications for ourselves and for each other. We had two choices as far as we both could tell: we could allow ourselves to be crushed by the weight of what was to come, or we could continually shift our focus onto the now. It was a profound realization, to live in the moment. I didn't take to it easily, but the option to think too far ahead was terrifying.

When the Grim Reaper comes cruising into your reality, he leaves an ominous warning that every moment could be your last. "Staying present" was no longer an obnoxious yoga instruction; it was a necessity, and it had the resplendent consequence of turning the world into a remarkable cornucopia. There was a renewed sense of beauty and wonder in my everyday experiences. I began to pay attention to everything: the sky and its Turner-esque displays of beauty, the way the birds glided effortlessly on the wind, the sheer explosive joy of our little dog's greeting after every excursion, the magnificence of a thunderstorm and the exquisite artistry of every flower. I paused to savour every sip of my morning coffee, held Everleigh as if she would melt away, kissed Jesse just because I could and I said "thank you" as many times as I could conceivably manage.

Chapter 36

MEDIATION OUTFIT

My cancer appointments rolled into each other, making the days indistinguishable. Jesse's schedule manoeuvred around the hospital visits for months on end. In between the doctor's visits the time arrived for him to be confronted by his victim. Daniel had told him that it was nothing short of a miracle she was willing to speak to him, and a highlight of his career that he'd managed to keep Jesse out of jail. He had a long-standing relationship with the judge, a progressive-minded fellow who was keen to see if this case could be resolved with communication. The court had leaned towards rehabilitation and restorative justice over punishment and our liberal government was inclined to favour the approach, particularly on charges related to drug use. I imagined that if he wasn't a straight white male, the outcome would've been radically different, even in a city like Toronto, where we wore our badges of inclusion with pride and flew the flag of diversity every day of the week. I knew and Jesse knew that we were living proof of privilege.

I realized that even though we had mounting debts and no money left in the bank, at least we had the option go into debt in order to pay the lawyer. What if we had no means of raising those funds? What if we had no access to a crackerjack lawyer at all? Maybe I could even be grateful for the debt, for the things it allowed us to do.

Every situation gave me the opportunity to reframe my reality. I would have to look at every adversity like it was a Rubik's cube, like there were multiple colourful combinations, some of which I simply hadn't noticed.

Jesse was instructed to meet the mediation team and his victim on a weekday evening in the core of the city. We talked about what he should wear, what he should say, how he needed to behave. I had suggested he listen more than speak and give her the possibility of healing by validating the trauma he had caused. It didn't matter from her perspective that he had lost his mind because of a drug. It didn't matter that he didn't mean it, that it wasn't his intention. It didn't matter that ordinarily he wasn't like that. His intentions, his reasoning, his logic, even his feelings, none of it mattered. He just needed to acknowledge her distress and apologize. He had altered her life forever, changed the way she felt and moved about in the world, perhaps caused PTSD, nightmares, heart palpitations and extreme anxiety I imagined at the very least. Her family would also be changed, the way she parented her children, the way she connected to her husband — it would all have been tainted by the shadow of that night.

Jesse had been fundamentally changed too. He had seen a drug counsellor, a psychiatrist and had tried to make amends by volunteering at a local charity. He had consciously tried to make his impact on the people he met a positive one, to be calmer, more present, more attentive, more thoughtful. When driving he was more inclined to avoid the aggressive drivers rather than engage with them. It was a perfect reflection of his internal evolution. He had finally stepped into the arena with his demons and instead of battling with them ferociously, he had invited them to take a seat and begin a dialogue about why they were there in the first place.

That evening Everleigh was having a sleepover down the hall at Marlowe's and when Jesse left I stood alone in our loft and I prayed. Not a prayer that religion would necessarily approve of, but a heartfelt request for Jesse to find the words he needed and for healing to begin for both of them. A drifting calmness came over me and I felt an inexplicable contentment, a peacefulness, a knowing that it would be okay.

Jesse arrived home late that evening. The meeting had gone well, he explained. I wanted to press him for every fine detail: what was the room like, what was she like, what did she wear, was she scared of him, did he listen, did he cry, did she cry, what did they say to each other, who started the conversation? I knew that my thirst for information would have caused him to retreat. I must not be excitable, anxious to know everything. I must give him the space to speak when he's ready. I listened with the acute all-consuming awareness of a field mouse anticipating the swooping wing of a predator. What transpired in this meeting would have profound consequences and I wanted a sense of relief that lay beyond hope.

He began and I got the feeling that he could feel my carousel of questions. "I mostly listened. She told me she didn't want to be there. That I was lucky I wasn't in jail, but the judge had asked her to try mediation. She knew I'd lost my job and that you had cancer and said she felt I'd been punished quite a bit and that she was sorry you were sick. She knew that I was typically a nice guy because she has friends who live here, neighbours that know us. She told me she was surprised we hadn't moved out. She told me what I'd done to her, that her husband had had to take a week off work to take care of her, that she needed several hair appointments to repair the damage I'd caused ripping her hair out."

I felt my throat catch. I had felt so sickened by what he had done. I was grateful to her that she was willing to be in the same room as him. I was grateful to him that he was willing to take it all in.

His victim had been advised by understandably outraged friends to take the charges to civil court, but she had decided against further legal action and instead handed Jesse a bill for a sum of money that would bury us in more debt. He took the document outlining her expenses and was grateful that his acceptance of the costs could lead to the closing chapter of their story. I was also grateful. She was entitled to every penny. His assault had led to therapy bills, repairing her hair, lost wages for her and her husband. The cost to her was far greater than a sum of money and we had both felt that she should be compensated however she saw fit.

The mediators had congratulated them both for being present and for being a shining example of effective mediation. Jesse had rejected their praise for himself and reiterated that his victim was the one who deserved the credit. Mr Hyde had finally been held accountable. If I'm being honest, part of me was envious that his victim was given a supportive forum and professional support to confront his abuse. But my fleeting envy was trivial in the grand scheme of it all. I would stay focused on my gratitude for the new and improved, 2.0, upgraded Jesse. I would silently thank his victim for her courage and wish her healing. I fantasized about the two of them delivering talks to high-schoolers about the dangers and consequences of drug use. I knew my imaginary, utopian world would never materialize, but I had control of my inner storyline and I would write, "They all lived happily ever after" in the final chapter.

Chapter 37

STARCHED APRON

It was October, Thanksgiving weekend. We were going to spend it at Shane and Violet's with Jesse's mum and stepdad. We arrived on the Friday afternoon in our overstuffed car, with Everleigh and our little dog crammed between the bags in the back seat. Food and drink had been packed neatly into coolers, clothing for any type of weather and our own pillows tucked under our arms. On arrival, we flung open the doors of the car, always grateful to have made the journey in under two hours. The dogs greeted each other like they were reuniting after years of torturous separation. Blue, the gargantuan Shepherd-cross, and the three-legged mutt, Tig, bounding about as our tiny little beast rocketed between their paws. Their wild enthusiasm always made us laugh.

We settled our things into the basement and retreated to the glorious back garden with a cold drink. The warm sun was beating down, uncharacteristic for October weather, and the huge expanse of lawn was still a vibrant green and not yet the dreary winter colour palette when everything became brown and grey. Jesse and I took a seat under the gazebo as Everleigh ran, jumped and cartwheeled on the grass with the blissfully happy pack of dogs at her heels. We watched with a quiet sense of delight, soothed by the happy-go-lucky spirit of a joyful child and playful dogs. We had just settled into this contented feeling when Jesse's phone rang. It was Daniel. He pinned his phone between shoulder and ear and quickly moved out of Everleigh's earshot.

As Jesse stood calmly in the furthest corner of the garden I heard the sound of tires in the driveway and I assumed my in-laws had arrived. I was glad to have a reason for leaving Jesse to his call, and went inside to investigate. My mother-in-law had said very little about his incident, but I was of the impression she would've slapped him across the face had she had the opportunity. Despite the anger that we had all felt towards Jesse, he was still our Jesse, father, husband, son, brother, and he was more than his mistakes, even his devastating mistakes.

I poked my head through the back door and decided against adding to the crowding in the little entranceway. Jesse's mum and her husband were fanatically organized, a skill set Everleigh and I both appreciated. They arrived with as much stuff as we had, but they would likely have an itemized, inventory list, I mused to myself. Their drive was more than twice the length of ours, but they never arrived exhausted and thirsting for tea like my parents would have. In terms of scale, the UK could fit into Canada approximately forty-four times; long drives were just part of being Canadian. My in-laws immediately set to work arranging their belongings and packing food in the fridge.

I went back outside and caught the end of Jesse's conversation with Daniel. As he finished the call, everyone spilled out of the house and into the garden. No one was aware that life-changing information was being exchanged. I delivered the customary hugs with gratitude, happy to belong to this family, happy to be outside on a beautiful sunny day, happy to be alive.

We gathered under the gazebo and soon Violet was ushering snacks and drink top-ups into the garden. She was an attentive host who loved to entertain and keep her guests happy. I always thought she would have been more at home in the 1950s, a contented suburban housewife, impeccably dressed, with a starched apron on top of her coordinated blouse and skirt, martini glass and cigarette perfectly perched between her long, elegant fingers.

I knew that there was news from Daniel, but I had decided to stay in this moment, listening to the conversation, sipping on my cocktail, watching Everleigh and the dogs play. I breathed it all in and sat, content, grateful, unfettered from the terror that had loomed on the fringes of each day.

A few hours later, Jesse and I found a quiet moment inside the house and he relayed the message from Daniel.

"I have to go to court on Tuesday, 9 a.m."

I interrupted, "Jesse, please, just tell me if this is good news or bad news? I don't think my heart can handle the suspense right now."

He put his hands on my shoulders, "Good," he said eagerly, "It's good news."

I felt the air returning to the room.

"I have to go to court with a certified cheque for the damages. Once I hand over the payment, it's over. They'll close the case."

We learned that his victim had been empowered by the judge to recommend Jesse be sent to jail if she was dissatisfied with the mediation. I felt so relieved not to have known our future had rested on the outcome of their meeting just a few days ago. It was almost a full year since this trial had begun and on Tuesday it would be over. All we had to do was find another stack of money and make sure Jesse arrived in court on Tuesday morning.

PART III:
THE REPAIR

It isn't an empirical truth that 'everything happens for a reason', but without ascribing some kind of meaning to tragedy it feels as though we're at the mercy of a cruel and unjust roll of the dice

Chapter 38

SUIT AND TIE

The Thanksgiving weekend passed with particular significance. We had savoured every meal, appreciated the company of people we loved and basked in the relief of knowing Jesse wasn't going to jail. We drove home early on Monday to ready ourselves for his court appearance on Tuesday.

Jesse's journey that Tuesday morning wasn't without incident. There had been a newsworthy car accident that had blocked traffic in every direction, and all routes to the courthouse were gridlocked for miles. A teenager had car-jacked an SUV and went for an early morning joy ride through the city. A high-speed chase had ensued and attracted the media like bees to a honey pot. Jesse negotiated with an obliging local resident to let him park in their drive-way and ran to the courthouse, sprinting between houses and through a park. He also had the added pressure of getting to the bank and arranging another line of credit to pay the damages. The entire morning devolved at break-neck speed, chaos bursting around him like exploding soap bubbles. It seemed like a fitting end to such a wild and unpredictable chapter in his life.

He arrived at the courthouse, five minutes late and marginally dishevelled. The proceedings were unfolding within minutes of his arrival. The crown had announced they were satisfied with the doctor's reports and his drug counsellor's evaluation. Furthermore, if the victim no longer wished to prosecute, then they too would be dropping the charges. The judge had declared the case closed. He was free to go. It was over.

The following morning we had an appointment with my oncologist. I was scheduled to have the picc line inserted into my arm on Thursday and chemo would begin Friday. Knowing that Jesse would be with me for the treatment would help me walk through fire. As we drove to the hospital I remembered a psychology term "counterfactual thinking", our human proclivity to muse about the multiple outcomes of any given scenario. I contemplated being a single parent, sick and unable to function, having no income and a husband in jail. It was heart-stopping to consider how things could have played out.

The previous few weeks had brought a steady stream of considerate gestures. As if each loving kindness were parcelled in exquisite gift wrap and delivered on bended knee. It was overwhelming. Every token of thoughtfulness was like a holy blessing, an unseen cleansing with mystical characteristics, like tiny particles of glittering light dancing blissfully into the inner darkness.

Jesse and I made our way through the plywood construction maze up to the oncology floor. The waiting room was always filled with men and women that looked to be at least two decades older than I was. I wondered how their bodies would weather the onslaught of poison that would be driven through their veins. I felt somewhat fortified by the knowledge that I was strong. The fanatical years I had spent at the gym trying to outrun the realities of my former marriage were paying some modest dividends. We settled into a corner, tip-toeing our way around the walkers and canes and waited for my name to be called.

Dr Thompson was apologetic as we made our way into her office. "I just had your file in my hand. Take a seat, gosh, forgive me, I seem to be very disorganized this morning."

I was still floating on the news that Jesse was free and was therefore unconcerned about my missing file or being kept waiting.

"Don't stress at all," I assured her. "We're not in a hurry."

Even the militant ticking timer in the parking lot, gobbling money as we waited, didn't bother me.

"I am so sorry," she repeated, "I've just worked ten days straight and I suppose it's starting to show!"

Her tone was convivial, but I was reminded that even those who hold our lives in their hands have vulnerable days where the treadmill wears them down. She darted in and out of her office, eventually returning with a medium brown folder clutched to her chest.

Her dark hair slightly tousled in every direction, she pushed the unruly strands aside and plopped her dainty frame into her chair. She sighed, then flashed me her perfect broad smile, "I have good news."

Dr Thompson proceeded to open the folder lying in front of us. I sat to the side of her desk that was pushed against the wall. I glanced at Jesse then back at Dr Thompson, "Okay, great! I love good news."

Not for a second did I imagine she was going to say what she said next.

Chapter 39

EMPTY POCKETS

D r Thompson pushed a piece of paper from my file across the desk. As if she were my teacher explaining the series of graphics on the page, she wielded her pen around and landed on the number seventeen, circled it repeatedly and said: "We're not doing chemo."

Jesse sat in the chair expressionless, as if he hadn't heard what she'd said. I looked back and forth between them, my head like a ping-pong ball, trying to take in the information, trying to make sense of the page in front of me, trying to gauge Jesse's response, trying to figure out if I had heard her right. She continued to circle the number seventeen as if she were hoping to hypnotically draw my attention to the number. It took some time for me to find the words and they came out in slow motion, "We're ... not? ... We're NOT ... doing chemo?"

My eyes began to well up. I looked back at Jesse, "We're not doing chemo," I told him.

He was still motionless.

With tears in my eyes, I reached out my arms to Dr Thompson, who reciprocated with a generous hug and laughingly said, "Ok, now I'm gonna cry."

I loved the humanity of this doctor, her open-hearted kindness and sincerity, her willingness to be proven wrong about the treatment regimen, despite her experience, despite the probabilities. She had put her own ego aside and taken the time to order an expensive test with the most marginal possibility of a good result. I was the outlier, the magical unicorn statistic. Perhaps my results would bring about more awareness and offer hope to the legions of patients behind me.

We returned to the paper in front of me and she began to explain the series of graphics and data.

"This number, seventeen, tells me everything I need to know; If your number is twenty or higher, we start chemo. Based on your pathology, I would've bet your number was going to be at least above twenty, probably twenty-three, twenty-four. But as you can see, it's well below the limit we have to satisfy in order to justify rounds of treatment. It means that if we did start chemo it would be less than two percent effective."

Her pen jumped to another number and graphic on the page.

"I mean, it's unheard of this result. I've been doing this a long time and it just never happens." Her smile never waned as she continued to jump her pen, wand-like, across the page.

The little office seemed to vibrate with excitable, jubilant atoms, crashing into my body, setting my skin ablaze with luminescent joy. Dr Thompson leapt from her seat to order me my own fresh copy of the results to take home.

"I'll cancel the picc line insertion and the chemo appointment. You just have to contact radiation. Who's your doctor?"

"Dr Sully," I replied.

"Right. Okay, I'll let him know, but you should get in touch so you can start radiation therapy sooner rather than later. I'll be giving you your other meds, hormone blockers — since your tumours were estrogen receptive we're essentially going to trick your body into menopause and shut down your estrogen supply. Let me talk to radiation about the best time to start those."

She scribbled notes in my file and then began to list all the side-effects of the drug I would need to take for the next five years. I sat on the edge of my chair, smiling and nodding like a bobble-head ornament. If she'd told me I would grow green hair from my nostrils I wouldn't have cared, I wasn't going to go through chemo.

Jesse seemed remarkably unaffected by the news. I wondered if part of him had simply unplugged from life in general, disassociating his emotional responses as a coping mechanism to endure the past year. It didn't matter; I knew eventually the information would land. In the meantime, I wanted to call my parents. I virtually skipped down the hall of the oncology floor, a grin on my face that must have made me look deranged, given the setting. Jesse dug his hands into his pockets and instructed me to wait at the main entrance.

"Shit. I can't find the ticket."

He patted down every pocket in search of the parking ticket we needed to leave the lot. I didn't care. It would be a costly fee if he couldn't find it, but whatever. I was going to survive this cancer. I was going to survive life.

I couldn't wait to call my folks and was scrambling around in my overcrowded bag for my phone to video call them. I reached the main entrance of the hospital and because I couldn't hold all the bits and pieces in my arms and simultaneously make a phone call, I crouched inelegantly on the ground and dumped everything on the concrete in front of me. I didn't care that passers-by might think it odd. I didn't care about the optics of anything much in that moment. Jesse marched towards the parking lot, his hands still fumbling around in his pockets looking for the elusive ticket. Standing in the same spot I had waited with a brand-new baby Everleigh almost exactly ten years earlier, I got on the phone to finally deliver some good news. I could barely see my parents on my tiny, smudged screen in the glaring sunlight, "Hi! Can you hear me okay? I'm at the hospital, you can probably see. I've got good news! I've got really good news!"

"What?!" my mother exclaimed, "For God's sake, WHAT?!"

I grinned like a Cheshire cat, "Do you remember me telling you about this test that they only do in California? The test that tells the doctors how effective chemotherapy will be?"

"Yesssss …"

"Okay, well I had to see my oncologist this morning and to be honest I hadn't even realised it was an appointment about the results. I thought it was just another pre-chemo chat or something … Jesus, I don't know what I thought the appointment was about really."

I was enjoying drawing out the first bit of happy news we had shared in so long. But I thought she might reach through the screen and strangle me at that point. Her eyes were fixated on me like giant cartoon eyes as if she was going to see an actual speech bubble appear out of my head.

"So, where was I?" I said, still grinning, "OH YEAH! I don't have to have chemo!"

She stared back at me for a beat. Surprising people with good news is never like it is on an episode of Friends, the actor's faces perfectly reflecting their internal cheerful glee. In real life people look more stunned than happy. I repeated more slowly, "I don't have to have chemo!"

The words began to sink in. "What?! Oh my god. Oh my god. Oh my god."

"I know! Can you believe it?! I'm a magical unicorn statistic! I'm a walking medical miracle! I mean, it's been twenty-four hours of life-changing good news. Jesse's not going to jail and I'm not gonna die. Not yet anyway."

We laughed.

"I just can't quite believe how fast things have turned around for you," she said.

"I was kinda hoping a miracle was going to just pop into our orbit. It's been such a wild ride I'm just absolutely ecstatic that we get to live a somewhat 'normal' existence for a while."

I wrapped up the call, giving my giddy parents the Coles' notes on Dr Thompson's explanation of the test results and some details about my new treatment program.

I saw our car emerging from the dark concrete entrance of the parking garage and I gathered my jumble of belongings off the ground. When I climbed into the front seat Jesse was still in a strange mood. Having paid the maximum charge for a lost ticket, he was distracted by the annoyance of it. I wanted to bring him back to the moment of such life-altering news. To unhook him from the triviality of everyday irritations and bask and revel in the outcomes of the last twenty-four hours. He had been freed from a lifetime of regret and consequences by not having to go to jail, I had been freed from the next year of my body and mind being dangled over the precipice between life and death. This was a magical moment, a perfect conclusion on the heels of Thanksgiving. I was very thankful indeed.

We drove home with the sunlight saturating the cinnamon-coloured interior, the sky a cerulean blue, offering a stunning contrast between inside and out. A harmony of colour was singing to me, asking me to notice, to pay attention, to look here and now and not throw my thoughts into the chaos of an unknown future.

When we arrived home, I met neighbours in the hallways and in an almost delirious sing-song voice declared to everyone I met that I didn't have to have chemo. A family who'd moved in recently were leaving for a walk with their newborn. The mum had tears in her eyes when she heard my news and we hugged in the hallway. It was these moments, the tiny capsules of human connection, filled with a powerful concoction of love, humanity, compassion and joy that I must swallow whole and remember forever. That was the medicine of life.

Chapter 40

HALLOWEEN COSTUME

My parents had decided to fly in before discovering I didn't need chemo, and we had all agreed that they should come anyway, despite the fact that we wouldn't need as much help. It was a show of support, the kind they had always given me, the kind of support that turns love from a noun into a verb.

People are kinder when you have cancer. They ask, "How can I help?" or say, "Please let me know if I can do anything." But speaking my needs was like speaking a foreign language for me. The words were awkward and fell clumsily off my tongue. Requiring help ran counter to the ingrained value systems so many of us were raised in, to be strong, to be independent, self-sufficient.

Help was best offered with specificity, such as, "Can I do your grocery shopping for you?" or, "How about I walk the dog this week?" I had decided that brochures on cancer needed to include a training manual for friends and family — what to say, what not to say, how to provide support and offer pragmatic help.

When we met my parents at the airport they greeted me with slight surprise, a reaction I had become accustomed to. I looked too healthy and energetic to have cancer. Aside from the slight limitations imposed by my surgery, I was visibly strong and bright-eyed. It had made me wonder how many others were just like me, dealing with life threatening conditions but going about their daily lives with no outward evidence on display.

My healthy appearance had caused people to remark on it and some, I had felt, to have an edge of scepticism, as if to imply I had made it all up. An unnerving realization that also gave me access to my own biases. How many times had I cast judgement on people not knowing what was happening in their bodies, in their minds, in their lives? My inner world and outer appearance did not reflect each other. How many millions were walking beside me with similar burdens no one would ever recognize?

A kindly neighbour across the street had offered up their rental house at a greatly reduced rate so my folks would have their own space for some of their visit. We lived in such a remarkable community, there was always someone willing to help, assuming I had the courage to ask.

We returned from the airport and helped my folks settle into the townhouse. I had collected some necessities from the grocery store and stocked the fridge. Jesse hauled cases up flights of stairs, Everleigh and Jet bounded from floor to floor, exploring three levels of living space. It was ordinary life in motion, and it filled me with joy.

Halloween was approaching, and I had engineered a costume for Everleigh that would take a family effort to construct. We would build together, work together, create together, be together, making something ridiculous and fun that would get recycled at the end of it all. Perhaps it was a metaphor for life. Would we get recycled? Come back as something wild and outrageous and fun? Choose our costume and see how the world responded?

Chapter 41

NOSE CLIPS AND SNORKELS

With Jesse's legal troubles behind him a new energy permeated our day-to-day experiences. We were more relaxed, more hopeful and even more optimistic about our future, especially since I had miraculously dodged the chemo bullet. I would still have to face multiple rounds of radiation, but that felt like it was going to be a cakewalk compared to being poisoned every week.

I scheduled my appointments. My body would be blasted with radioactive particles in six precisely targeted areas so any remaining cancer cells would be obliterated. The treatments would take place every day, Monday to Friday, for three weeks. I may be nauseated, extremely tired and depressed. In fact, I might experience a litany of side effects that were par for the course with all cancer treatments.

My parents trailed along with me for the first appointment. About ten minutes away from my usual hospital, the sprawling mini city of Sunnybrook Hospital was a maze of one-way roads, flanked by towering named and numbered buildings. The constant stream of traffic and people moving around and in and out seemed like a National Geographic time-lapse of an ant colony. It was intimidating and overwhelming.

I had learned to seek out the volunteers, gently smiling seniors with kindly eyes and all the patience in the world. Whenever I met them I felt like I wanted to fall into their arms, then beg them to come and hold my hand during treatments. I wished that hospitals had hand-holders on call. During one of my appointments with Dr Mahoney, her nurse had held my hand while the horse-sized needle was injected into my skin expander. It was a tiny gesture of thoughtful care and consideration. It said, simply, but powerfully, I'm with you, I've got you, it's okay.

The first appointment was in a darkened basement area of the hospital. It felt a bit like we were walking into Frankenstein's lab. We wandered down the linoleum-lined dingy hallways under the aging fluorescent lights into an even darker cave-like waiting room. We were the only people there, which made it feel slightly apocalyptic. I had half expected to be greeted by a one-eyed, twitching mutant human the result of being over-exposed to the pre-war cancer treatment of radium. I was so glad to have access to modern medicine.

The set-up appointment for radiation was over an hour. It was supposed to last about twenty minutes. There are multiple methods to secure a patient for treatment and the key is to find a way for the patient not to move an inch while the machine blasts its very targeted laser beams into the body. This isn't as simple as it sounds. The body has to be so precisely positioned and the patient must hold the exact pose for about twenty minutes. No sneezing, no coughing, no big breaths, and god forbid you have gas.

The first method involved lying on an uncomfortable MRI table in an even more uncomfortable contraption designed to hold my arm very still. Holding this contortion for over twenty minutes in a room that felt like ten degrees below freezing required a certain amount of detachment and mental focus, and a fair bit of internal swearing.

The young nurse repositioned my body in micro-movements, dozens of times over. When I was in the final pose, feeling like a fish on a marble slab, the nurse returned from the viewing area and announced, "So, this isn't going to work because the radiation points are too close to your heart in this position."

The second method involved having to hold my breath for fifteen seconds, three times, with precisely the same inhale/exhale exchange. "You have got to be shitting me" I had thought, but smiled politely nonetheless. This was going to be very interesting. I had had breathing issues since I was a small child. Croup was a common occurrence and I have several memories of holding my head over a bucket of steam with a towel draped over me so my airway would relent and open up a little. As an adult, the whiff of a cold would often result in my breathing sounding like a ninety-year-old chronic smoker and trying to breathe was like trying to suck a lung-full of air through a pinhole sized straw. I had found a very convenient first aid solution in my industrial grade steamer I hauled to work with me, a virtually instant steam bath I could blast into my face – carefully, so as not to peel off a layer of skin. Needless to say, such precise regulation of my breathing whilst lying on the MRI table, contorted into a pretzel and freezing cold, was well beyond my skill level.

My rather exasperated nurse was doing her best to be patient and I couldn't help apologizing and telling her how much I appreciated her efforts. I also knew that I would be the one on the slab every day and I would regret gritting my teeth and not disclosing any discomfort. She proceeded to haul out a nose clip and snorkel type contraption, telling me it would help with my breathing. My eyes must have looked like the cartoon eyes that pop out of the head on springs. I tried to explain,

"To be honest …" I began awkwardly, "I'm not sure this is going to work either. I have a dry throat and my airway is … anyway... ok let's try!"

As soon as my nose was clamped shut and the hard rubber mouthpiece was being gripped by my teeth it was game over, I couldn't get enough air into my uncooperative airway. At that point I wondered what other contraptions might be next out of the closet.

After conferring with her colleagues my nurse disappeared and returned with what I later described to my folks as a NASA beanbag. A bright purple malleable form that they could push around my contorted body into a type of brace that would hold me still. It was like a spa treatment compared with the other methods. I would have to climb in and out of this human taco shell for every appointment and, with the help of the nurses, position myself in precisely the same way every day. "This is more like it!" I had thought, "what took them so long to haul out the five-star treatment?" I had assumed this was a last resort for a number of reasons, the cost and the storage of a human sized taco shell being the most obvious.

The set-up appointment had also involved getting my first tattoos, six tiny dots that would permanently mark my skin with the target points for the radiation machine. Only the one administered in my armpit was noteworthy, and mainly because it had to be repeated a few times to be visible.

I left Sunnybrook with my folks still patiently in tow and went to my next appointment at my regular hospital to see my cancer surgeon, Dr McDonald. The Sunnybrook technicians had used multiple coloured sharpies to draw on my body, a series of circles with crosses and dots and X's. Dr McDonald examined me and said,

"Oh, they really marked you up at Sunnybrook."

"No." I replied, "I just decided to join a cult."

Without missing a beat, she bounced back, "Ah, not a prison gang then?"

We smiled and I enjoyed the easiness of her presence and delighted in the feeling that everything would be okay.

Chapter 42

CLOSET CULLING

The holiday season drifted by like a quiet early morning mist. We said goodbye to my folks in early December and fell into an almost normal routine once more. I finished my radiation treatments before Christmas and aside from an itchy, unsightly burn, I was outwardly no different.

By January I had another schedule of hospital appointments and was notified they had discovered a small anomaly on my right breast. As if I had drained every reserve of shock, I was unperturbed by the news. Part detached compartmentalization, part surrender to the unknown had become my new intake filter. They would need to investigate further by scheduling an MRI, which couldn't be achieved as I had an implant with a two-inch metal port embedded in my left breast. I would have to wait until my surgery was scheduled in June and hope that whatever might be lurking in the tissues of my chest would turn out to be nothing of consequence.

Despite the notion that my health might be sitting on an open ledge for an unknown amount of time, our greatest stress was financial. We had relied on bank loans and some generous donations from family to help us through. We had both hated being in such a helpless position, unable to meet our financial obligations and having to rely on the kindness of others. I had previously had judgments about how people got into such debt; it had always seemed irresponsible or careless. But I had a very different perspective now. I now knew how it could happen virtually overnight and in many cases it happened when people were simply trying to do the right thing, perhaps paying medical bills for family members or bailing your loved ones out of a legal situation. I had very little judgment left in me about anything anymore. It had been replaced with deep compassion and a willingness to understand beyond the scope of my own experiences.

As our lives returned to an almost normal pace and routine, we re-evaluated everything we were doing and decided we would try to pull the plug on our urban life. I wanted to make a clean break and head back to England, where I still felt an inexplicable draw. I would take Everleigh with me and ask my parents to let us stay a while until we could land on our feet. I was excited to get Everleigh into the UK school system, which was leagues ahead of the heavily unionised Canadian system in terms of accommodating neuro-diverse kids. I had no idea how it was all going to unfold but I needed to try to make a life there and if I could make it work then Jesse would come along. If, on the other hand, he was able to find work outside of the city then we would come back. It was a contest to see who could build us a better life in which place. It was also a slightly mad plan, but I had to follow my gut instinct.

We decided we should rent out our apartment. It would give us some relief from our mortgage payments and allow us some time to gather our thoughts. We could find more secure work without such pressure and put our stress load on hiatus. We also wanted relief from the city crowds, the traffic, the constant hum of a thriving metropolis. We wanted to walk on trails, dip our feet in lakes, breathe crisp morning air and feel the sun on our shoulders.

We wanted to be together as a family, to explore the new boundaries of our marriage. A marriage that had been pushed to the very limits of tolerance only to find deep love and profound understanding. We wanted Everleigh to grow up knowing her parents could navigate uncertainty, survive adversity and model resilience. We wanted all the things beyond what the world had deemed necessary for a happy life. Our job titles, our status, our bank accounts, our possessions — all had fallen into a greyscale of unimportance. We were alive. We were free. We were together.

We busied ourselves with preparing our loft for tenants. Jamming our storage locker with our personal belongings and selling or re-homing an absurd number of things.

"I never want to have this much stuff again." I said to Jesse as I loaded another cart for drop-off. There was an immense freedom that came with offloading our possessions. Like we were culling the weight of our lives into prioritized compartments: needed, not needed, must go, why do we even have this?

As we paired down our lives, Everleigh and I kept aside our essential belongings we would take to the UK. The lightness of getting rid of so much stuff certainly had a psychological and even a spiritual impact. I was glad to have a sense of simplification about everything. Organisational guru Marie Kondo was definitely onto something profound; physical clutter is mental clutter and vice versa.

I had already visited the school I wanted Everleigh to attend when I was scoping out Sheffield university. It was a small Catholic school in the Yorkshire countryside. My deceased and beloved grandparents had been devout Catholics, and when we visited the school a little over a year earlier, I had the strangest sensation that my grandmother was there in those hallways, smiling and nodding as the children meandered the corridors.

When the decision was made to send Everleigh to the school, the head teacher had told us they had one opening available. One opening in the entire school, and it happened to be in the year that we needed. I wondered once again if the Universe was whispering, "I see you. It's okay."

Or, maybe it was just a happy coincidence.

Some kind of deep faith had taken root in me. Faith not in religion, not in

God, not in anything I could easily explain. Perhaps it was just the faith of knowing we can survive more than we can imagine when adversity comes clawing at our door. Perhaps it was the result of walking the path of resilience. Perhaps it was because I had no choice but to make it through the last few months. Perhaps it was because pessimism wasn't an option and I had doggedly insisted my inner voice speak as often as possible of gratitude and joy. To love more openly and without armour. To express words of encouragement, understanding and compassion, to myself and to others. To refuse to indulge in mindless complaining, or subject myself to the monotony of bad news, frightening statistics or unnerving information. I had been disciplined with my inner dialogue and reached for love over fear whenever I could manage it.

It had helped me survive the hurricane that had been our lives, not because I was better than any other human, but because I had very few options. I wasn't brave for going through cancer; I was afraid, but I learned to breathe and let go a little. I wasn't happy-go-lucky at every turn; I was a sobbing, crumbling mess at times. I wasn't stoic or resilient every time the phone rang with bad news; I thought I would collapse. But I didn't, because ultimately I had no choice. I gave myself no choice. Life was going to continue to serve up a river of twisting, turning, churning circumstances and I was going to learn to swim in it.

Chapter 43

SCHOOL UNIFORM

Everleigh and I arrived in England in late February of 2020. We landed on a predictably damp and cool winter day with a short-term plan and a couple of lightweight suitcases. I would go back to Canada for surgery in June and hoped that between now and then Jesse and I would have a tenant in place and a clearer vision for our future.

Planning ahead is a luxury not everyone is afforded. If you don't know where your next meal is coming from, who cares about what might happen next week? There is an urgency to each moment that must be attended to. If you think your life will be cut short, there's no pleasure in thinking too far down the line. Besides, my life view had shifted permanently, from projecting and planning and goal-making to trying to stay present in the now.

We were asked all the reasonable questions by friends and family: Where will you live? How will you live? What are you going to do for work? What about Everleigh?

Unable to provide satisfactory answers, our lives were in a holding pattern, like planes queuing on a runway waiting to take off, but heading to an unknown destination. It was difficult to explain that we didn't have much of a plan, that we were content to let the chips fall where they may. It seemed irresponsible, reckless even. But we had come through such a turbulent part of our lives that not only was planning too far into the future exhausting, it seemed somewhat redundant. We'd been blown open by the unpredictability of the last sixteen months, and to orient ourselves back into a normal routine we needed to take one day at a time.

We bundled our cases into the trunk of the taxi and began the two-hour drive to my parent's little stone cottage in the Yorkshire countryside. It was a relief to be in the fold of safety, of predictability, of love and acceptance. It was a place where I didn't have to explain myself, where I was understood, where I was valued and seen. Where my mother's home cooking would be served up daily and the comfort of it would soften the knife's edge of unease. It would be home for the next five months, and I would discover just how much I missed Jesse.

We arrived on a Friday and Everleigh would start her new school on Monday. She was scared about everything and vehemently opposed to wearing "an ugly uniform". I had done my best to placate her fears and sell her on the merits of a uniform. But she had every reason to be afraid; it was a new school, new friends, a new teacher, a tougher curriculum. She had plenty to be concerned about and my voice wasn't much of an antidote to her rising anxiety.

When Monday morning arrived my mother and I walked her through the stone archway of the little hundred-year-old schoolhouse. We were greeted by the broad and assuring smile of her teacher, Mr Dixon, who had handed off his class so he could introduce himself properly and give her a full tour of the school. I reflected on my own first days. There were nine in all, and not one of them had acknowledged the fear and feeling of being overwhelmed that typically accompanies a new student. There had perhaps been a class introduction from the teacher, a perfunctory "this is the new girl, kids", but it was clear that I was alone to figure it all out. Everleigh, on the other hand, had the advantage of a wiser education system and a more sensitive approach where her well-being would be paramount.

She trailed after Mr Dixon, who bounded from room to room in his red converse sneakers, cracking jokes and asking her questions about Canada.

"We have about a hundred and fifty students here. Everleigh, how many were in your school in Canada?"

"Six hundred," she announced, as if it loaned her street-cred.

I already loved this teacher. He connected with Everleigh right away. He spoke to her with respect and compassion, and he was having fun, the critical component to offset anxiety. She was acknowledged by every teacher on her tour and reassured that they would all look out for her. One of the fifteen members of staff was a learning mentor, a woman who had herself transferred from Scotland to England as a child and knew the fear of such universal change. She introduced herself and asked Everleigh if she would like to come to the office at lunchtime to use the phone and call me, just to let me know how she was doing. Even parents had chatted with us in the hallways and told us they too had attended the school as children and that she would be well taken care of. Unlike her Canadian school, where the kids ran boisterously helter-skelter to class, bursting through doorways and shoving their way past parents, these children walked politely by us, bidding us "good morning" and holding open doors. I joked that any minute the birds and squirrels would launch into a welcome song and sprinkle flowers across our path.

I silently thanked my grandmother as we tagged along for the tour and I knew that her spirit would also be watching over Everleigh. This place would nurture her and keep her safe. We left that morning with the same sense of peaceful knowing that can't be logically explained or rationally understood.

Chapter 44

LOUNGEWEAR

It was three weeks into our stay when reports of a global pandemic began to make headline news. At first we had wondered what all the fuss was about — surely this would be like a bad flu and we would just wash our hands a little more often? But the virus ripped across the planet and Jesse sent me a message to say that Canada had been put on lockdown, the population quarantined and ordered to shelter in place. Britain was carrying on with life as usual, but ominous warnings had been fired from other countries and we hovered over our laptops and cell phones waiting for the inevitable news to descend.

Covid-19 clawed its way through Europe, and Britain's leadership had left much of the population infuriated at its slow and ineffective response. There was a strange atmosphere across the country; people were scared and the messaging from government and world leadership was contradictory. The world was collapsing and frantically trying to mitigate the fallout. Over the ensuing three months, workers were furloughed, schools were closed indefinitely, businesses shuttered and we all became cemented indoors, trapped with uncertainty and anxiety, bedfellows who make a mockery of even the most grounded people. Once again we faced the fear of life-changing unknowns, but this time it was alongside the entire planet.

As I watched the rest of the world anxiously try to create a new reality as their daily lives became unravelled, I felt as if I had already been through the training, knowing that when crisis hits, bullshit stops. I kept a routine for myself and Everleigh. I knew that being anchored to some kind of schedule was essential, that I would have to be disciplined not only with my time, but with my thoughts. Keeping the fear-mongers at bay takes a certain awareness, monitoring the external influences of the media and realizing how insidious a steady stream of negativity can impact both mind and body. We would need to be sensible and practical. I would always have an eye trained on the proximity of fear, the wrecking ball to happiness.

I had come to understand that happiness is a habit. It isn't the external thrill of a new pair of shoes or a beautiful home. Sure, those things could bring fleeting happiness. But long-lasting happiness was nothing to do with external things; it was developed internally, like a muscle, thoughts being the dumb-bells. Lifting them day by day would re-shape the mind.

I had become like an annoying ex-smoker, the ones who cannot tolerate the presence of smoke, who unapologetically flap their arms dramatically should they encounter the cloud of a cast-off cigarette. Except it wasn't smoke I disapproved of — it was whining, complaining, telling stories of how we had been slighted. Amplifying the injustices of our day by repeating them to anyone who would listen. My distaste for it was evident in my silence, my lack of participation with the complainer. I had become acutely aware of how the retelling of daily injustices would accumulate in our minds, eventually block-ing the possibility of joy. I had no issues about a good kvetch now and again, but mindless complaining was different. It had staying power.

Sometimes I liked to geek-out on psychology data. One of my favourites was the notion that of the thousands of thoughts we think in a day, 80% are negative, 95% are repetitive. Which made me consider not only the origin of thought, but the seeming lack of control and deliberate, conscious shaping of our thoughts.

How is it that we could fly to the moon but had not yet learned to harness the power of thought? We hadn't even scratched the surface of a discussion around the importance of learning to direct the way we think. Most of us run an unconscious loop of negative drivel and made-up storylines that don't even exist.

Not that I was any kind of thought guru, but I had been through enough catastrophe that I had become acutely aware of how my thoughts impact my emotions. Our thoughts even have physical consequences. We can imagine the sourness of sucking a lemon, for example, and then with a little effort of imagination produce additional saliva as if we were actually having the experience. The body's chemical factory is intertwined with thought and programmed to respond to it with incredible reliability. It's in the gap between external stimulus and response where I had learned to find my own power — I learned to pause, breathe, observe the chemistry flowing through my body and let it ride out.

One the most useful phrases I'd learned during therapy was: "What I make up about that is …" It was a mental checkpoint to stop my assumptions about a person or a situation and mine the accuracy of where my thoughts were headed. I had been guilty many times over of creating a narrative that didn't exist, or one that was wildly inaccurate because my own inner filters were damaged or utterly skewed.

This realization had helped Jesse and me clarify and defuse a myriad of sparky little moments that had the potential to light up a completely unnecessary row. These tiny moments of checking in with each other were wrapped in curious inquiry instead of resentful assumptions. An honesty and kindness had developed between us that hadn't existed before. If he snapped at me I would simply say, "I don't like it when you snap at me. It makes me anxious."

Because of this revised response, I would discover that he had just wanted to do something the "right way" or had put unnecessary pressure on himself and had responded from that emotion. He wasn't responding to me, per se, but to the narrative running in his own mind. It was a bit of a Dalai Lama moment in our relationship.

I imagined our thoughts like bubbles of energy, loaded with an inky, swirling mess of coloured light, some black and dark, others bright and vibrant. If we unleashed the energy within the thought, its contents were free to leak out and seep into other thought bubbles. I wondered if we would ever be able to "see" thoughts and measure their "energy". Did they even have energy?

As the pandemic raged through the world the only thing we seemed to have control over was our own inner musings. Hospitals cancelled all manner of routine checks and surgeries in preparation for the urgent demands of Covid. My own surgery was no exception. It was cancelled, and I wondered if the little dot that needed an MRI would be gleefully growing into another tumour, an unchecked bully having its malevolent way with my cells. I cruised through the weeks and months of lockdown trying not to pay it too much attention, constantly shifting my focus back to what was right in front of me. Get up, work out, make breakfast — the treadmill of a daily routine provided a scaffold for sanity.

Prospective tenants for our apartment all but disappeared and we decided we should sell our loft, take away the strain of its unrelenting costs and put some money back in the coffers. I couldn't think of selling it without some heartbreak, but it was a drain on us and I would have to have faith that we would find another home we loved as much. I would need to ensure faith was my constant companion, bridging the gap between unhinging fear and anchoring hope. This is where mental health battles were waged, in the delicate threads between uncertainty and hope.

I wished I could have shared some faith with the world, breathe some hope and peace over the collective heartbreak. The fear was palpable, not just for the patients who developed the terrifying symptoms of this deadly disease, but people with medical issues that weren't related to the virus. That was a group of people whose needs would be benched indefinitely. There were men, women and children, who were newly diagnosed with cancer and had all their life-saving treatments put on hold. The anxiety it must have created for the patients and their families was unimaginable. Contemplating the devastating consequences of being sick during a pandemic caused me to feel so grateful that my cancer had occurred when it did, when I could be surrounded by my family and get to my appointments unhindered. Being confronted by a life-changing illness is earth-shattering as it is, but the complication of facing a diagnosis in the middle of a global pandemic would be truly unhinging.

All manner of institutions were collapsing around the world and we were forced to consider new ways of conducting business, new ways of learning and new ways of connecting. It was fascinating to watch such rapid adaptation, that for some resulted in an improved way of life, for others it was devastating. Everleigh had loved shifting into online learning and found it much easier to focus in her quiet little nook with her teacher on call via a private screen. But we were extremely lucky, we were a household of three adults and one child with enough physical space for her to have her own desk and an iPad to herself. There were families all over the world without the space or technology to accommodate a child trying to learn from home. There were parents trying to juggle the demands of their jobs from their kitchen table as well as try to keep their children enrolled in some kind of learning activity. I knew plenty of families with multiple young children, some without access to an outdoor space, I couldn't contemplate the pressure-cooker these poor families must have been in. It was an impossible task for many, which resulted in women with children under the age of ten quitting their jobs at a disproportionate rate compared to other working groups. But once again, it gave me pause to reflect on just how privileged my circumstances were at the moment, how grateful I was to have survived a year-long trauma and land feet-first in the swirl of an international crisis.

It was also fascinating to watch the rise in popularity of certain products – food and alcohol, loungewear and sweatpants, craft-related products and home-improvement supplies, trampolines and garden sheds. We were eager to fill our lives with activities we could do from home and many of us over-stocked our fridges with indulgent snacks. I began to refer to my burgeoning weight as my Covid-19 pounds. I wasn't alone in my unwanted weight, but it was a relatively trivial consequence of our slow, meandering days. Unlike the consequences of being trapped in a house with an alcoholic.

Jesse had often walked a fine line between sobriety and alcoholic, not the kind of alcoholic that needed a daily fix, but the kind that would binge drink themselves into such a state that they couldn't recall things the next day. I remembered the uneasy feelings I had stewed in when Jesse and I were at a family function, a wedding or a party, and I spent most of the evening with one eye trained on his alcohol intake. It was a foregone conclusion that as the night progressed Jesse would push the scales of happily tipsy into belligerent drunk. A pit would grow in my stomach as he became more and more intoxi-cated and inevitably turn his increasingly antagonistic behaviour on me.

There was a pivotal moment on a trip to Jamacia that he had spat out a litany of hateful comments, his face contorted with anger, raging inches away from me. I couldn't say or do anything to reason with him, I would just have to let it ride out until he sobered up. That feeling of despair, helplessness, anger and then resentment would be the cycle of emotions I would be left with. On that occasion in Jamacia, the next morning I had dressed for breakfast and as I was about to leave Jesse stirred and asked where I was going. "Away from you" I had replied, and his face looked bewildered and hurt. When I recited his vitriolic words back to him, he was shocked. He had no recollection of any of it. But then there was an apology, a heartfelt apology and I knew that was a turning point, or at least the beginning of the turn. New and improved Jesse had been to parties since without over-indulging and I was gradually letting go of my anxious anticipation that things would go sideways.

For the people who could not escape their abuser the lockdown would have dire consequences. There was an upsurge of domestic violence and a significant increase in the UK of third-party calls to police. Most likely because more people were at home and could hear the plight of their neighbours.

The world was on its knees, as we had been and in its own reckoning of epic proportion. All pain and injustice would be amplified, called into question and reviewed with merciless scrutiny. Covid-19 was putting our lives in a vice and in many cases, forcing us to put right what had been blatantly wrong. I knew that such a rapid and condensed shift in our daily lives would be crushing, and I knew that we would prevail. Like the flower that forces its way through concrete slabs, it will fight its way towards daylight, towards growth, towards survival. The Universe whispering to the seed, "Grow here, this way, rest, breathe, relax, it's okay, over here ... that's right, follow the light."

One afternoon, gathered with my parents around the patio table in the back garden, an idea occurred to me. The kind of idea that suddenly explodes into being, just like the flower through concrete, a colourful flash of unexpected joy, a wild and crazy expression of growth that couldn't be ignored. We were finishing our lunch and taking in the unusually sunny day, watching the birds glide and swoop across the farmer's field and listening to the bees buzzing hastily from flower to flower. It was serene and content, the type of fertile atmosphere that good ideas like to germinate in.

"I think I should buy a campervan," I announced. "Jesse and I could use it as our space here, you know, parked in the driveway, so we can stay out of the house. It could be our home base while we're here and when Everleigh's done school every six weeks, we'll go to Europe or visit some family here."

My parents both smiled and I knew the idea was inspired, dropped into my mind by that unknown force, delivered with a celestial bow, a "Ta-Dah!" moment from the Universe.

Inspired ideas are generally the ones that make everyone smile when announced. They are simple and elegant solutions that require little effort to understand. They arrive when the mind is calm, or better yet, when the mind is content and free from trauma. When there is room for thought processes beyond survival. This alone would be reason enough for me to set my sights on being happy — it was the gateway to well-being, the panacea to struggle, it made room for solutions and wiped away confusion. It had come back to me, the quiet inner voice that was always available, but simply easier to find when in a state of relaxation. That voice came from intuition, or meditation, or arrived via the lyrics of a song, or a passage in a book, or while we are playing, or singing, or painting, or dancing, or running. It could be heard in multitudinous ways. We just had to be in receiving mode, however we could get there, with whatever method our soul required.

Jesse loved the idea of a gap year, touring my homeland and exploring together in a cozy little nest on wheels. Everleigh oscillated between excitement for the adventure and grief in leaving her childhood home. We sold our apartment about two weeks after it went on the market, a slow sale under normal circumstances, a small miracle in a global pandemic. We were cautious about announcing our plans to certain people. I was nervous about the judgment. I had been told years ago that I was "too old for adventure" and that my wanderlust was "irresponsible and selfish". Besides, I didn't want anyone to rain on our parade. We needed this change, and a time-out from big responsibilities. We needed a complete break from the last sixteen months of struggle and trauma, a place we could literally escape from it all.

Chapter 45

WEAR ELASTICATED PANTS

The long and languishing days of quarantine had smacked our plans into yet another unexpected turn, but with acceptance of what is and without struggle blocking the way, there appeared a previously unforeseen opportunity.

I casually decided to join a creative writing group where my mother volunteered. The group was led by a woman who was undoubtedly meant to be in my orbit. She encouraged me to write about my experience with cancer. I wrote a poem and she facilitated it being published on a Sheffield University website. That tiny step was just enough encouragement to allow me to write this memoir. I marvelled at the serendipity of events, of this woman being in my life via video conferencing, cheerleading my writing efforts, helping me overcome the crippling self-doubt of perfectionism.

This woman, with her wisdom and insight and endless support, teased the words from within my soul and gave me permission to pour all the pain, the struggle, the uncertainty and the unknown into this story. This story that ends with the knowing that when our lives are burned to the ground, pure possibility presents itself. When dying becomes a reality, living is all we want to do. When chaos tears through time we find a way to stand still. When we are on the edge, the brink, the precipice, that's where we come face-to-face with the life force that lives in all of us.

Just breathe, my fellow broken soul, just breathe.

Chapter 46

BOXING GLOVES — FROM JESSE

I don't consider myself a bad person, but that really depends on who you ask. My wife thought I was a monster, because she saw the monster in me. My mother always thought I was a menace, even though she loved and nurtured me.

I was never a fan of resorting to violence, but when I grew up there seemed to be no other option. I was a tall kid, a big kid, and became a man with a very noticeable physical presence. As such, I was frequently targeted. It might have been by the school bully in the playground, (always the new kid as our military family relocated every four years, I was easy to spot). I was perceived as an alpha male, a trophy if I could be taken down, dominated, slayed. I could be standing in a bar, minding my own business, and suddenly be confronted by a drunken idiot wanting to fight me. It was a pattern I'd known all my life. But over time it became a chicken-and-egg conundrum. Which came first, the violence perpetrated on me, or the violence that grew inside me, which I inflicted on others?

My inner tough-guy had his advantages, too. He was a menacing comrade who would defend me, protect me, keep me safe. But he'd also run amok, a wild uncontrollable beast I ultimately couldn't seem to contain. He had put me into plenty of situations where I might have ended up dead. Anger grew inside me like a swollen festering wound, eventually becoming a mess so debilitating I couldn't even acknowledge it existed.

I had internalized all the violence over the years — normalized it even. At times I even bragged about how many times I'd been in handcuffs, tossed in a cell or obliterated an opponent. It was disgusting. It wasn't me. Except it was. It was part of me that would be dragged from its cave and blown to smithereens in what would become that night of cruel, fucked-up misadventure.

Being a man in today's world is confusing, destructive, and in need of serious self-diagnosis. I have always been perceived as an alpha, but nowadays, I don't even know what that means. I know it's not the outdated definition of a stoic and aloof protector or aggressor. It's going to be up to each man individually to create a definition that brings about a better world, builds better relationships, models vulnerability and doesn't call it weakness. We're one decision away from a different definition and it begins with men like me. Men who need to take a seat, take a hard look inside and learn to wrap their struggles and fears around language rather than letting intense emotion explode through their fists.

Confronting the darkness in me can be painful and lonely at times, which is why I eventually decided to join a men's mental health group in the UK – Andy's Man Club. An initiative originally founded to encourage men to come together and talk about their problems and in so doing help to lower the suicide rate. Although I'm a new member I feel certain I can use my experiences and mistakes to help support and encourage other men to reach out, to be there for someone and give my own pain a purpose.

I can't change my past, no matter how much I want to. No matter how big the ache of regret for the things I've done, the choices I've made. But I can try again. I can re-write my inner dialogue any time I choose. I made a promise to myself, to my family, to complete strangers, to take a pause, to be more reflective, to be less reactive, to be better, try harder. I want to inflict joy, not pain, on the people I love. The time for change is now.

Acknowledgments

Special thanks to my long-suffering editor, Wendy Morley,
who gave me the ultimate gift of confidence to share this story.

Matt Lowe Designs, for his painstaking evaluation of colour,
form and font choice that created this gorgeous cover.

The Sunday Times bestselling author, Catherine Cooper, who very kindly
turned her hand to the back cover copy and helped me refine and reorganise the
message.
The generosity of women in business is beautiful.

My incredible parents, who encouraged me to make this story public
so we can help others know they aren't alone in struggle.

My husband, who has been the greatest cheerleader of this book and whose
bravery in sharing such a dark moment has also given me courage. He is an
extraordinary person who wants to help me end the stigma of addiction and the
families impacted by it.

To our daughter, we are blessed to have such an evolved little soul to love.
We're so sorry for all our mistakes — big and small.
We promise to continue to work on ourselves. We love you.

Rachel was born in a small mining town in South Wales to a single parent in the 1970s. After decades of moving from place to place, she found her long-term home in Toronto, Canada, where she carved herself a 23-year career as a wardrobe and interior stylist, appearing in glossy magazines and on television fashion spots. In 2020 she sold everything and crossed back over the Atlantic with husband and young daughter in tow. She now lives in South Yorkshire, has traded her designer heels for hiking boots and no longer rubs shoulders with celebrities, instead volunteering to help people with their mental health.

Printed in Great Britain
by Amazon

25525026R00136